High School Underachievers

Sage Series on Individual Differences and Development

Robert Plomin, *Series Editor*

The purpose of the Sage Series on Individual Differences and Development is to provide a forum for a new wave of research that focuses on individual differences in behavioral development. A powerful theory of development must be able to explain individual differences, rather than just average developmental trends, if for no other reason than that large differences among individuals exist for all aspects of development. Variance—the very standard deviation—represents a major part of the phenomenon to be explained. There are three other reasons for studying individual differences in development: First, developmental issues of greatest relevance to society are issues of individual differences. Second, descriptions and explanations of normative aspects of development bear no necessary relationship to those of individual differences in development. Third, questions concerning the processes underlying individual differences in development are more easily answered than questions concerning the origins of normative aspects of development.

Editorial Board

Books in This Series

High School Underachievers

Robert B. McCall
Cynthia Evahn
Lynn Kratzer

**Individual
Differences
and
Development
Series**
VOLUME 1

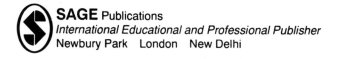

SAGE Publications
International Educational and Professional Publisher
Newbury Park   London   New Delhi

For information address:

SAGE Publications, Inc.
2455 Teller Road
Newbury Park, California 91320

SAGE Publications Ltd.
6 Bonhill Street
London EC2A 4PU
United Kingdom

SAGE Publications India Pvt. Ltd.
M-32 Market
Greater Kailash I
New Delhi 110 048 India

Printed in the United States of America

Library of Congress Cataloging-in-Publication Data

McCall, Robert B., 1940-
    High school underachievers : what do they achieve as adults? /
Robert B. McCall, Cynthia Evahn, Lynn Kratzer.
        p. cm. — (Individual differences and development ; vol. 1)
    Includes bibliographical references (p.   ) and index.
    ISBN 0-8039-4604-X (cl). — ISBN 0-8039-4605-8 (pb)
    1. Underachievers—United States. 2. Underachievement—United
States—Psychological aspects. 3. Personality and academic
achievement. I. Evahn, Cynthia. II. Kratzer, Lynn. III. Series.
LC4691.M32   1992
371.95'6—dc20   92-2842
                                                                    CIP

92 93 94   10 9 8 7 6 5 4 3 2 1

Sage Production Editor: Judith L. Hunter

Contents

Tables and Figures

Acknowledgments

The authors are indebted to Drs. Gordon McCloskey, Walter Slocum, and William Rushing, who collected the high school data in 1965-1966 while at Washington State University with funds provided by the University and the Office of Education. Further, we appreciate the extensive cooperation of the Career Development Study; Luther B. Otto, Project Director; and Vaughn R. A. Call and Kenneth I. Spenner, Project Associates, who collected the follow-up data with support provided by the Boys Town Center and the National Institute of Education (NIE-G-79-0046).

The analyses reported in this book were conducted at Father Flanagan's Boys Home with financial support from Boys Town and from The William T. Grant Foundation of New York (85-1048-85). The preparation of the manuscript was partly supported by the University of Pittsburgh Office of Child Development with funds from the University.

The authors appreciate the comments of Kenneth Spenner and Mark Appelbaum on a portion of an earlier draft of this manuscript, and we thank Diane Heurta, Heather Fisher, Catherine Kelley, Kathy Whitmore, and Judy Maringo for help preparing the manuscript.

To all seriously underachieving adolescents, who live with the gnawing dual fears of failure and of success, and whose feelings of helplessness and incompetence limit their potential in our society and their personal happiness; and to their parents, especially those who agonize and weep over their youths' bewildering disparity between ability and performance, and who only want to help them, but can't.

Series Editor's Preface

It is especially appropriate for the Sage Series on Individual Differences in Development to be launched with a book by Robert B. McCall, along with his colleagues C. Evahn and L. Kratzer. For the past two decades, Professor McCall has been a leader among developmentalists. His theoretical and methodological concerns have shaped the field, and can be summarized in the following "McCall to arms": (a) individual differences as well as average developmental trends, (b) "naturalistic" development as well as experimental manipulation, (c) longitudinal as well as cross-sectional designs, and (d) change as well as continuity. This book instantiates and validates his credo.

Professor McCall is clearly a trendsetter. At a time when fashion favored experimental descriptions of average performance at different ages, he emphasized the need for studying individual differences using naturalistic and longitudinal designs, emphasizing change as well as continuity. The field followed his lead on each point. Now the study of underachievement is not as fashionable as it was in the days of Sputnik, but Professor McCall may again be leading the way, this time toward renewed interest in underachievement as our society shows concern about steady declines in the school performance of children in America.

Underachievement in school is clearly an issue of devastating importance for children, their parents, and society, despite difficulties in defining and assessing the construct. Two great strengths of this book, which focuses on outcome rather than process, are its systematic use of two unique comparison groups of children and its long-term longitudinal design. The comparison groups include children with the same grades or the same mental ability but who are not underachievers. This allows McCall to disentangle underachievement from low achievement in his attempt to describe what characteristics distinguish underachievers. It is astonishing that until now there have been no long-term follow-up studies of underachieving children into adulthood. Only with such research can we see the real-world consequences in education, occupation, and marriage. Thirteen years after the original assessment as juniors in high school, more than 88% of the sample was reinterviewed. In addition, this is the largest and broadest study of underachievement ever reported, with follow-up data on more than 5,000 individuals covering the entire range of ability.

McCall's research suggests than on average, underachievement in high school casts a long shadow. However, the results are not entirely bleak. Some children break away from the shadow, "catching up to their ability," as McCall puts it.

Professor McCall is a gifted writer, always writing with great clarity and verve. His special contribution has been communicating research to scientists in other fields, parents, teachers, family service professionals, and the general public. This talent serves him well in presenting the results of his own research and in showing us what we know and don't know about the important problem of underachievement.

ROBERT PLOMIN

Prologue

An underachiever is a child or youth who performs more poorly in school than would be
expected on the basis of his or her ability. How underachievers have
been defined and the extent and nature of society's interest in them
has changed over the last decades.

A Very Brief History

One can rarely find the word *underachiever* in the educational literature before the middle 1950s (Shoff, 1984). Perhaps this is because it
was not until then that the measurement and prediction of ability and
achievement were refined or accepted (Fine, 1967), and because social
and political interest had not focused on the problem. But in 1957, for
example, the Soviets lofted the first satellite, followed shortly by a U.S.
failure to duplicate that feat. As a consequence, concern arose over
U.S. technological ability, and it was alleged that the nation was not
doing enough educationally for its most capable students, many of
whom were performing at mediocre levels in school. Social, political,
and educational attention focused on the so-called gifted under-

achiever—the pupil of superior intelligence who performed much more poorly in school than expected.

In the 1980s, educational attention had shifted toward children who do not perform well in school because of specific disabilities—e.g., learning disabilities, attention deficit disorder—and on children who simply do not learn basic minimum competencies. Educational and scholarly interest has been diffused across a variety of low-achieving circumstances.

There appears to be two current foci of interest. One is directed at the educationally disadvantaged, usually urban and often minority youths, who derive very little from their school experience. This is the educational issue of and societal concern over minimum competency and basic literacy. These youths may or may not be underachievers by the technical definition of that term used here. That is, a disparity between measures of ability and measures of school performance may or may not characterize all such youths, but it is assumed that these young people could do better in school. They are, in a sense, *presumed underachievers* at the lower end of the ability scale.

The other focus is directed by middle- and upper-middle-class parents who set a high value on education and have a low tolerance for mediocre performance by their children or the schools. These are among the parents of "true" underachievers as defined here. They use national chains of private tutoring (e.g., Sylvan Learning Center, Hutchison Learning Center) and private psychological counseling (e.g., Motivation Development Institute) services. They call and are called by teachers, administrators, and counselors. Some researchers speculate that today's Yuppie parents may be prime candidates for rearing underachieving children. They value education highly, delay childbearing until after tasting the occupational and financial fruits of their own academic success, and invest their parenting energies in only one or at most two children who must "have it all," just as they are attempting to do. Certainly, if they produce an underachiever, they will be most likely to be concerned and want to do something about it.

The educational issue has thus broadened from its narrow focus on the gifted to poorly achieving students across the ability range. Although the study of underachievement per se has almost disappeared, the problem continues. There exist no studies of under-achievers across the entire range of abilities, nor any serious follow-up studies of such students.

One reason for the lack of contemporary studies is that scientific research on underachievers is messy. The concept of underachievement itself is untidy (e.g., if one can underachieve, is it possible to "overachieve" one's abilities?), no unassailable methodologies exist for studying underachievers, the technical considerations in conducting research on this topic are daunting, and the scientific literature on the problem is confusing. Much of this book will be devoted to dealing with these issues of scholarly interest.

But the heart of this book is an attempt to answer two very concrete and practical questions: Does underachievement exist as an actual, clinical syndrome that makes some youths different from non-under-achieving youths with either the same ability or the same grades? And what happens educationally, occupationally, and maritally to under-achievers after they leave school?

Many parents, if not scientists, know the answer to the first question and fear the answer to the second: they know their youngsters are underachieving and they know the children are different. No scientist, as some have maintained, can convince these parents that their youths' behavior is nothing more than an "error of prediction." And most of these concerned parents seriously doubt a school counselor who tells them that their youngsters will get their educational "act together" once they leave home for college.

Three Cases of Underachievement

Parents of underachievers describe their youths in many terms, all linked by a commonality: The children do not try, at least not as hard, as consistently, or as persistently as they could. Three such cases are described below (from McCall, 1983). They represent the concrete reality of underachievement that motivated and guided this research, and the concerns they represent should not be lost in the academic detail that pervades many of the chapters that follow.

Mr. and Mrs. Landis are both professionals who value education highly and sincerely care about their son, Ken. Mr. Landis tells about Ken's lack of confidence beginning when the boy was in junior high, and Ken's fear of failure and rebelliousness as well as about the parents' trial-and-error attempts to deal with the problem.

Mr. Landis: We didn't know anything was wrong until we received a midterm report. Ken was getting Fs and Ds. We didn't expect straight As, but there's nothing wrong with Ken's head. He's not brilliant, but he's certainly capable of Bs.

We know how important school performance is to a youngster's future, but Ken couldn't care less. "School's dumb, it's prison," he'd say.

We had a special conference with his teachers. The problem was he simply had done nothing. He turned in no homework and made no effort in class. One teacher suggested we just let him fail, repeat the grade, and allow the natural consequences to take effect. Sometimes I think that is the right approach, but frankly neither of us has the patience for that.

Our first impulse was to lay down the law. "I'm going to see to it that you do your homework before any television." So I sat in his room with the books and just said, "I'm here to help you with your homework whenever you want to get started." I waited in deafening silence while he just stared at the wall. Personally forcing him to do his homework just didn't work. He's too rebellious.

So we instituted a daily report card. Every day Ken had to have each of his teachers initial his assignment book, testifying that all homework from last night was turned in and that Ken had recorded correctly all the details of the next assignment and the next test. In addition, we tried to get off his back, at least a little. The rule was that he could do what he wanted after school, but after dinner, it was homework—period.

The first thing that happened was that he did nothing the first night or two. Eventually he got tired of being alone in his room. Then, he would dash off anything and call it done. So we required that we check it over and that it be done correctly. Later, after things seemed to improve, one teacher said he had never seen the assignment book, although he had apparently signed it. Forgery! The little devil. No wonder he hadn't improved his grade in that course. So, we both talked with him and explained that if he wanted independence he had to earn our trust. Of course, we also checked with his teachers occasionally, and we told him we would. That stopped the forgeries.

Occasionally, he seemed to try to fail, or maybe he was trying to make us mad. He would do the homework, for example, then "lose" it.

After several months, we found that he enjoyed having us help him with his homework. He had us chained to him for 2 to 3 hours a night. So we made sure he knew how to do an assignment, then left until it was time to check it over. We also promised to pay for each grade point of improvement and for any Cs or better, so grades, not just homework, became the criterion.

Well, he finished the last quarter with all Cs. He's capable of better, but that's about as much improvement as I think we could reasonably expect in three quarters.

We've spent many nights in bed trying to explain to the darkness why this happened and what Ken's problem is. I've decided it's several things.

First, Delores and I are both in education and we were both honors students. Ken's younger sister is straight A. So, although we never told Ken what grades we thought he should get, I guess he figured perfection was expected.

Second, Ken has decided he can't meet those standards. He told Delores one night during a bedtime chat that we "shouldn't have adopted a dummy" like him. We all cried over that.

Third, his strategy for dealing with an impossible standard is to not try at all. I guess he feels that he hasn't failed if he hasn't tried.

Fourth, we are fairly pushy parents. We want our children to do certain things, and we nag too much. Ken's sister handles this well, but Ken wants his independence. He's told us that in many ways. So he gains independence by resisting school and homework, which are things we want him to do.

THE CHADWICK FAMILY

Rod was hyperactive in elementary school. After this problem diminished, he used it as an excuse not to study and his parents accepted it. The Chadwicks remember the long process of change.

Mrs. Chadwick: In kindergarten, Rod was diagnosed by doctors as hyperactive and above average in intelligence. When he reached junior high, we began to realize that he could settle down and pay more attention to things, but actually he seldom did. For example, I had heard that hyperactive children didn't do well in math, so I just accepted poor performance in math. He would simply say, "I can't do it. My mind doesn't understand such things." And I would accept that. Well, eventually we discovered that his mind does understand such things.

Back then he got Cs and Ds. He did the minimum in school, just enough to get by. In fact, he rarely did anything. He'd watch a lot of TV—maybe 5 or 6 hours each weekday. He did not read, he did not go out for sports, and he had very few friends.

We knew he was capable. Not only did his test scores say so, but whenever someone really took an interest in him—believed in him—he did fine. We have had him tutored several times, and he has always done much better with his tutors than in regular class.

Mr. Chadwick: But he had no sense of his future. We'd talk about what jobs he could or could not get if he continued to do poorly in school. In seventh grade, he didn't seem to care. Later, he figured he was going to become a mountaineer. He'd hunt, trap, live off the land, build a cabin on government property so he wouldn't have to pay taxes. He had figured out something he'd like to do that would not require education.

Every once in a while, Rod would let his ability shine through. For example, a month ago he had a big success at school. He chose to build a miniature battlefield as a school project. The project was worth 200 points, and the teacher gave him 250. It showed Rod that he could achieve if he wanted to.

Mrs. Chadwick: We tried everything to help Rod do this more often, including getting a psychologist who took 3 days to really get to know Rod. She discovered that he was using his energies to show the world that he couldn't do things, so he wouldn't have to do them.

Also, at that time I was into the nag syndrome. I would insist on Rod studying an hour every night, and then I would check up on him. It was nag, push, shove. I wasn't always consistent either. I can't believe how awful that was. But this psychologist told me that I was taking all the responsibility for him—I was almost taking all his tests for him. And he was letting me do it. So we began a system of "if this doesn't get done, then this will happen." It was a graduated thing. If you don't get your homework done satisfactorily by 8 p.m., then you'll have to clean the garage on Saturday, and then it was being grounded for the weekend.

That helped our relationship enormously. I didn't have to nag and criticize, plus we could be supportive, be on his side, and help him to get what *he* wanted. It boosted his self-confidence, which had been a real problem. We weren't always sensitive to that issue. All of us were top achievers. I can remember him saying, "You expect so much of me. You expect me to produce as much as Julie [his sister]. Well, I'm not like that." And he isn't—he's better, but not "cured."

I guess—it's terrible to say—but I guess I loved him if he would produce, or at least I must have given him that impression. He felt he was loved only if he met our standards—that's what was coming through. So I tried hard to love him right where he's at. When problems arise, I try to tell him that I love him even though I don't approve of what he's doing—that sort of thing. Oh, hindsight is wonderful.

THE LATIMER FAMILY

After her divorce, Karen Latimer moved to a new section of town with her son, an honors student who was a senior in high school, and her daughter, Candy, who was a few years younger. Candy turned to alcohol and drugs instead of studying, and Ms. Latimer took a very patient approach to the problem.

Mrs. Latimer: Candy has had a problem with school off and on since kindergarten. She gets bored very quickly. It depends on her teachers. If they keep her interested, she excels; if not, she tunes everything out.

When we moved, Candy started in her new school with a very positive attitude, but it quickly deteriorated. She felt school was too difficult. I told her, "Your new school isn't too hard: Your old school was too easy."

I tried to encourage her. "There isn't any grade in school you can't accomplish if you want to make the effort. You're a very smart girl." But she didn't believe it. I guess she thought I had put her way up high, and that she really wasn't that smart and couldn't live up to such high expectations. So she didn't care and did nothing.

A little later, her brother told me that Candy was taking alcohol and drugs. She got them on the school bus and was high by the time she arrived at school. I didn't want to confront her, like "You tell me exactly what you are doing and stop that sort of thing." I was afraid it would drive her even further into it. Recently, she said it probably would have had that effect.

So I watched her for several weeks. I tried to talk with her about drugs in general. You know, "So many kids are into pot and drugs these days, do you have any problems with these things?" She'd always say no. But she was like a yo-yo that year, way up or way down.

Then one summer night she and some friends got into the beer a bit heavily, and Candy came home violently sick. She said that was the last time. I hoped so, but it wasn't.

When school started again, she was real gung ho. "I'm really going to do well this year," she promised, "because so much of my future depends on high school." But soon she was failing at least one course, and the counselor called both of us in. Candy seemed like she wanted to try, but it was clear to me that something was bugging her. So I told her that she and I were going to have a big heart-to-heart that night.

I very calmly, yet lovingly, let her know that I knew she had been taking drugs. Her little face went, "You did?" And I told her, "I don't like it, but it's not going to affect my love for you." Tears streamed down her face. I guess it was the guilt that she had done something wrong and the fear that I would be disappointed in her. I tried to convince her that I understood those things. I said, "Hey, grandfather is a minister; I was raised very strict. There were things I did behind your grandmother's back, and I was scared to death that she wouldn't love me anymore if she found out. But Mom's love doesn't work that way."

Candy also said that she had done the drugs to be one of the group, to be accepted. I guess she felt that if she couldn't make good grades, she'd join the other crowd. Eventually, she decided she didn't need to do that. She is doing a bit better in school recently, but her grades are erratic—As through Ds—not as good as she could do, but better than she was doing before.

These three cases illustrate in concrete form the diversity of underachievers but also many of their common characteristics, which the remainder of this book will demonstrate are typical and, unfortunately, often persistent.

What Is Underachievement?

Underachievement, as the prologue suggests, is not a new phenomenon; given the definition we use in this book, there always have been and there always will be underachievers in any group of students. Scholars of educational issues have studied underachievement only episodically, however—mostly during the 1960s and 1970s—although concern seems to be rekindled today. What do we already know about this problem?

Our review of the literature in this and the next two chapters is representative, not exhaustive. Our concern is restricted to investigations of underachievers per se, and most of these studies come from the fields of special education, educational counseling, and clinical psychology. Our review does not cover the extensive literatures on general achievement behavior from psychology or on educational and occupational status attainment from sociology. For the most part, we paint broad strokes rather than fine detail.

Definitions

Both conceptual and operational definitions of underachievement are complicated and problematic.

TYPES OF UNDERACHIEVEMENT

Essentially everyone agrees on the commonplace, general definition of underachievement as it applies to education: The underachiever is a child who performs more poorly in school than one would expect on the basis of his or her mental abilities. The conceptual definition represents a discrepancy between actual and expected performance—a circumstance readily recognized and voiced by well-educated parents with children who do poorly in school. But scientists need greater specificity, and complications arise, for example, in categorizing the different types of underachievers.

Gifted versus nongifted underachievers. As indicated above, the modern study of underachievement initially focused on so-called gifted underachievers. Not surprising, then, was the early definition—which probably has been cited more frequently than any other—that "the underachiever with superior ability is one whose performance, as judged either by grades or achievement test scores, is significantly below his high measured or demonstrated aptitudes or potential for academic achievement" (Shaw & McCuen, 1960, p. 15). Many early authors emphasized high or superior mental ability in their definitions of underachievement, partly because interest in underachievers was kindled by the observation that many gifted students did not perform as well in school as one would expect. Today this concentration is diminishing, partly because contemporary social, political, and educational concern now focuses on low-achieving students regardless of ability. In any case, the past emphasis on one portion of the ability distribution raises methodological problems (see below and Thorndike, 1963) and renders comparisons across studies difficult or impossible.

Chronic versus situational underachievers. A distinction between chronic and situational underachievement also was made early (e.g., Fine, 1967; Fliegler, 1957; Miller, 1961; Shaw & McCuen, 1960). A *temporary* or *situational underachiever* is one whose academic performance temporarily declines below expectancy, often in response to personal or situational stress (e.g., divorce, a particular teacher, relocation). In contrast, a *chronic underachiever* displays the underachievement pattern consistently over a long period of time (Whitmore, 1980). Unfortunately, no specific length of time demarks chronic from temporary or situational underachievement. The research literature, however, focuses almost exclusively on what are seen as chronic underachievers, a tendency reinforced by Thorndike (1963), who suggested that a consistent pattern of underachievement was necessary to rule out the possibility that a deviation between ability and performance was simply random error (see below).

Hidden underachievement (Shaw & McCuen, 1960) refers to students who do not perform up to teacher expectations even though their grades and mental ability scores are not discrepant. For example, some students score poorly on ability tests and perform poorly in school, but display verbal fluency and an extent of knowledge that convince teachers that they are more capable than either their scores or their grades reflect. Other students with high mental ability achieve high grades, but teachers nevertheless judge them capable of performing better. Hidden underachievers are detected only in studies that include teacher judgments as well as test scores or grades to define underachievement, and these unstandardized measures of school performance further complicate comparisons across studies.

General versus specific underachievers. A distinction between *general* and *specific underachievers* has emerged recently (e.g., Whitmore, 1980), perhaps as a corollary to the rise in concern over specific learning disabilities. Whitmore (1980) divided the domain of underachievement into three parts: specific subject, particular area, and general. Some students, she observed, were underachievers only with respect to a single ability or subject. A child might be exceptionally able in mathematics, but perform no better in math classes than in other subject areas; or a student might perform well except in, say, algebra or foreign languages, presumably for motivational reasons. This type of underachievement has been little studied.

Some students underachieve only in a somewhat broader content area, such as science, mathematics, or language (i.e., reading, spelling, and language arts). As educational interest focuses on curricula in particular areas, increasing attention will be paid to such underachievers, although anecdotal reports by investigators searching for students who underachieve in one subject area (e.g., mathematics) suggest that specific underachievement may not be common (S. Nelson-Le Gall, personal communication, 1986).

The type of underachievement most commonly studied is *general* and not limited to particular subjects or subject areas. Few studies have systematically explored the breadth of underachievement, however, either across academic subjects or outside academics.

Underachievement versus learning disabilities. Shortly after the concept of underachievement was proposed, a distinction was made between nonlearners and nonproducers (Kessler, 1963). *Nonlearners* include, for example, children with identifiable learning disabilities who score substantially better on general measures of mental performance than they perform in the classroom. *Nonproducers,* on the contrary, display no obvious learning limitations, yet perform more poorly in school than would be expected on the basis of their ability scores. Presumably, their performance deficit is associated with motivational factors.

Generally, the literature on underachievement is more concerned with nonproducers than nonlearners; definitions of underachievement implicitly and sometimes explicitly exclude children who suffer from a learning impairment, presumably physical in nature, that produces general or specific performance deficits. And, of course, if a child is mentally retarded, presumably both ability and performance will be simultaneously and similarly low, and no discrepancy between ability and performance will exist.

Children with certain disabilities might usefully be classified as underachievers. A disability might interfere with the student's ability to cope with the procedures used in classroom instruction, but not with his or her performance on an assessment of ability. Attention deficit disorder, for example, is an identifiable characteristic that contributes to poor school performance, but may or may not be reflected in mental ability assessments. Some learning-disabled students suffer motivational problems that produce even poorer performance than would be expected with their disability taken into account, as was the case with Rod Chadwick in the prologue.

Such distinctions, however, are not commonly made in the studies we reviewed, partly because much of the literature on underachievers predates the contemporary interest in learning disabilities and partly because a major portion of the contemporary definition of learning disabilities is underachievement—that is, a discrepancy between general ability and general performance in school. Most studies of underachievers rely on the discrepancy between performance and ability; do not deliberately screen out the learning disabled; and focus on personality, motivational, parental, or classroom factors as causes of underachievement.

OPERATIONAL DEFINITIONS

The operational definition of underachievement produces more serious complications and less agreement among investigators than the conceptual definition. Annesley, Odhner, Madoff, and Chansky (1970); Asbury (1974); Dowdall and Colangelo (1982); and Farquhar and Payne (1964) found that operational definitions of underachievement varied so greatly that substantial percentages of students classified as underachievers by one investigator would not be so classified by another, rendering comparisons across studies impossible.

Measures of ability. Generally, investigators have used IQ tests, administered either individually or to groups, and tests of mental and educational "aptitude" to measure general mental ability. Achievement tests, although usually taken as measures of academic performance (see below), also have been used to estimate mental ability.

Conceptually, aptitude tests presumably reflect basic abilities necessary to learn something in the future, and achievement tests assess knowledge and skills that an individual has already acquired. But many theorists have argued that the distinction between aptitude and ability tests is more conceptual than real (Humphreys, 1974; Kaplan & Saccuzzo, 1982; Sternberg, 1982), and a number of studies in other contexts have used achievement scores and traditional IQs interchangeably (e.g., Runco & Pezdek, 1984; Wallach & Wing, 1969).

Empirically (see below), specific IQ tests, aptitude tests, and achievement tests intercorrelate within and between types at approximately the same level, and on this basis at least, all three could serve as estimates of mental ability (if achievement tests are not also used as a measure of performance). General achievement tests, although conceptually the least appealing of the three types, have the practical advantage that they are more commonly used in schools than IQ or aptitude tests and therefore are most likely to be used to identify underachievement in the field.

Typically, a single administration of a single instrument is used to assess mental ability. But Thorndike (1963) and others after him have argued for multiple predictors of ability administered repeatedly. This course can be especially crucial when gifted underachievers are the focus of study, because some mental gifts (e.g., creativity, the visual and performing arts, leadership) are not adequately reflected by scores on omnibus mental ability tests (Myers, 1980).

Measures of academic performance. The most common assessments of academic performance are by achievement tests and some form of grades (grade point average, rank in class, or grade level on an academic achievement test). Achievement tests have the advantage of being standardized and comparable across samples and subsamples (e.g., several schools within a single study), but they yield scores too similar to IQ or aptitude tests to produce a meaningful contrast. Grades lack standardization, but offer the practical and ecological utility of being the primary concern of educators, parents, and students.

Defining underachievement. In a few studies, teachers, parents, or the students themselves were simply asked if the student was an underachiever or they were asked to rate the degree of difference between a pupil's achievement and abilities. In most studies, however, some form of difference was calculated between an assessment of mental ability and an assessment of school performance. These several approaches were reviewed by Farquhar and Payne (1964), Annesley et al. (1970), Dowdall and Colangelo (1982), Thorndike (1963), Willson and Reynolds (1985), and Yule (1984). In comparisons between methods, subjects have been categorized differently for different measures of discrepancy. Annesley et al. (1970) compared four different methods of calculating discrepancy and found only 16 of 57 underachievers to be so designated by all four definitions; five of six pair-wise comparisons between methods produced statistically significant differences in classification.

Methods of defining the discrepancy between ability and achievement fall into three broad classes, with finer distinctions made by some reviewers (Farquhar & Payne, 1964). The first is to use *arbitrary absolute splits*, with underachievers defined to be higher than a certain minimum on a measure of mental ability, but lower than a certain maximum on a measure of school performance. This method is most commonly used by those interested in gifted underachievers, because it focuses on absolute levels of performance for each variable. Thus, Broman, Bien, and Shaughnessy (1985) defined their target group to include pupils with IQs greater than 90, but reading or spelling subtest scores on the Wide Range Achievement Test one or more years below grade level; Combs (1964) defined underachievers to have IQs greater than 115, but grade point averages below the top quartile of the distribution.

This method suffers the obvious liability of lacking generality and comparability from study to study, because absolute values of scores or rankings are totally dependent on the particular assessment scale or sample, with no agreement on what assessments or particular splits should be used. Further, selecting extreme segments of a distribution may capitalize on chance, including some students as underachievers because of random error rather than any psychological characteristic. Finally, the designation of who is an underachiever is related to the ability measure. Although intended by those who focus on gifted underachievers, this circumstance limits the applicability of the method for those who do not wish to focus on underachievers of a particular ability level.

Another measure of discrepancy is the *simple difference score,* which requires a common metric for ability and achievement (e.g., standard scores, grade level). Curry (1961) defined underachievement to be a discrepancy of at least 10 points between the *T* scores for the California Test of Mental Maturity and the California Achievement Test.

Calhoun (1956) looked at discrepancies greater than the average absolute differences in the sample between months attained on a mental ability test and months attained on an achievement test.

The simple difference score approach suffers from statistical problems. Relating the measure of discrepancy (i.e., underachievement) to the measure of ability tends to result in overestimating the number of underachievers among students of above-average ability and underestimating the number of underachievers among students of below-average ability (e.g., Reynolds, 1984; Willson & Reynolds, 1985). This bias derives from the fact that a simple difference score is basically a forced regression analysis with the regression line dictated to have a slope of 45 degrees. If the actual (i.e., unconstrained) regression of grades on mental ability has a slope of less than 45 degrees (which is likely), then students with large absolute differences between the two scores (i.e., high mental ability), but somewhat lower grades will be identified as underachievers by the simple difference method, but may fall close to the actual regression line. The reverse will be the case at the other end of the scatter plot. From another perspective, regression to the mean is likely. For two correlated variables, individuals who score high on one are not expected to score quite so high on the other, and those who score extremely low on one variable will not score quite as low on the other.

A second limitation is the substantial unreliability of difference scores. The reliability of a difference score is poorer the higher the reliabilities of the two assessments and the greater their correlation. For example, if the two reliabilities are .80 and .90 and the correlation between ability and performance is .70, then the difference scores will have a reliability of .51 (Thorndike, 1963). Therefore, the bias plus the unreliability of the simple difference score approach make its use problematic at best.

A third approach is to use a *regression method*, as we have done. Of the several procedures available, the most commonly used is the simplest and seemingly the best statistically (Willson & Reynolds, 1985). It consists of calculating the regression of the achievement measure on the ability measure, and then calculating the deviation of each subject's score from the regression line. Subjects with a large negative deviation are defined to be underachievers. Gowen (1957) and later Farquhar and Payne (1964) advocated using one standard error of estimate as the cutoff, and most subsequent studies using the regression approach have employed this criterion.

The simple regression approach avoids some of the disadvantages of the other methods. The discrepancies between expected and actual scores are independent of the predictor variable (i.e., mental ability), so the method can be applied across the entire range of mental ability without bias. Second, in some sense, the regression approach can be applied regardless of the particular measures involved, so it has some generality. Finally, although reliability remains a problem, deviations from a regression line have better reliability than simple difference scores.

The simple regression method has at least three limitations. First, it assumes the standard error of estimate is a constant value across the entire range of ability, which is unlikely. Second, the use of one standard error is arbitrary and lacks empirical justification. Third, the regression method will always produce a given percentage of underachievers in a sample. In *any* sample, defining as underachievers students who fall one standard deviation below the regression of grades on mental ability scores (an arbitrary cutoff value) will produce approximately 16% underachievers. The method thus obviates meaningful answers to questions about how many underachievers exist and when underachievement first appears (see below).

Does Underachievement Exist?

It is clear that the measures used and the way underachievement is defined make a substantial difference in who is designated an underachiever and in the observed correlates of the problem. A case can be made that underachievement, especially when defined by the regression method, is essentially artifact or error; from a purely statistical standpoint (Thorndike, 1963, 1971; Wood, 1984), defining underachievement in terms of regression deviations has been assailed as a curious enterprise at best.

Is it prediction error? Usually when one attempts to predict one variable from another, the interest focuses on the degree of prediction and the amount of variation in the criterion that is associated with or explained by the predictor. "To make capital out of what *cannot* be explained by giving it a label, in this case underachievement or overachievement, is certainly unusual. . . ." (Wood, 1984, p. 231).

Further, we usually relegate variation in the criterion that is not associated with the predictor to the status of error, so one must ask whether those who deviate (i.e., underachievers) are simply errors of prediction (Thorndike, 1963). Demonstrating otherwise is difficult, especially when the correlation between ability and achievement is high, thus reducing the reliability of the difference between actual achievement and expected or estimated achievement. It is for this reason that Thorndike (1963) and many after him have urged replication of the classification exercise. In practice, however, this is rarely done, but in one instance where it was, the stability of classification of severe underachievers was quite high (Maughan, Gray, & Rutter, 1985; Yule, 1973). As a substitute, investigation can be limited to extreme underachievers and their grades averaged over a substantial period of time, a strategy we used in the current study. It further helps to demonstrate consistent and meaningful psychological, educational, or other correlates of underachievement.

Other statistical problems. Thorndike (1963) also worried about the heterogeneity of the criterion. Grading practices, for example, differ among schools, so that a student of a given ability might become an underachiever at a very good school, but not at a poorer school. Nor is it appropriate to mix students who take harder courses with those who take easier ones, or males with females (girls typically have higher grade averages than boys). When such groups are combined in the same regression equation, the mean differences can produce a spurious regression or lead to classifying more of one category of students as underachievers than would otherwise be the case.

Another problem arises from the limited scope or accuracy of the predictor (Thorndike, 1963). Some ability measures are more accurate in forecasting achievement than others, and a combination of predictors entered into a multiple regression equation might correctly eliminate some students from being classified as underachievers. Although some pupils may be designated underachievers simply because of the imprecision or the narrowness of the predictor, very few studies use more than one predictor.

Conceptual oddities. Even the general concept of underachievement presents some logical problems. If underachievers exist, then perhaps "overachievers" do too, and the regression method of definition would certainly allow students who fall one standard error *above* the regression line to be identified as overachievers. But how can one logically achieve *better* than one's abilities? The very concept of ability connotes an upper limit beyond which one cannot achieve.

This issue is largely semantic, because the definition of under- and overachievement does not rest on performance substantially below or above *ability*, but rather substantially below or above *what would be expected or predicted on the basis of ability*. Although unpopular in some circles, the terms underachiever and overachiever will be used in this book because of their long-standing familiarity to both educators and parents.

Other problems with the concept are less easily dispatched. Implicit in the idea of underachievement is the notion that mental ability, however measured, is a fixed standard against which school performance can be evaluated. But Thorndike (1963) wondered why the opposite logic could not apply and school achievement become the standard. After all, the measures of ability are probably not much more reliable or valid than the measures of school performance. By this reverse logic, underachievers in the first case would now be called "overintelligent." Such problems with the concept of underachievement have led many educational and psychometric experts, from Thorndike (1963) to Cronbach (1990), to argue for its abandonment. Although these scholars make valid points, we believe a concept of underachievement does exist (see below), and we will present data to support this contention.

COMPARISON GROUPS

The literature mostly comprises studies describing the educational and psychological characteristics of underachievers and efforts to remedy their problems. Only a minority of studies include a comparison group of any kind, and when one is included, the comparison group is only loosely matched with the underachiever group.

Same MA, Same GPA. When a comparison is used, the most common approach is to contrast underachievers with a group of students with approximately the same mental ability, but performing at a level commensurate with that ability. This will be called a "Same MA" comparison. No previous studies have compared underachievers with students who are matched on school performance rather than on mental ability—a "Same GPA" comparison. We have used both comparison groups in our research.

To illustrate the limits of past studies, Combs (1964) defined underachievers to be students with IQs greater than 115, but grade point averages below the first quartile. His comparison group was composed of students with IQs greater than 115, but grade point averages above the median—a loosely defined Same MA comparison group that could have included members of the underachievement group. Seeking greater precision, Hummel and Sprinthall (1965) and O'Shea (1970) regressed grade point averages on ability test scores and defined underachievers as those with negative deviations from the regression greater than one standard error, overachievers as those with positive deviations from the regression line greater than one standard error, and "par achievers" as having discrepancies "close to zero" (Hummel & Sprinthall, 1965). A few studies have compared underachievers of various degrees—for example, Gowen (1957) selected groups of underachievers that varied in the extent to which their grades deviated from their ability scores. It is not clear in these studies whether the groups were similar in either MA or GPA.

Implications. The failure to include comparisons with students who have the same grades but who are not underachievers means that essentially the entire literature about underachievers and remedial programs for underachievers may not be uniquely related to *under-*achievement, but simply to *lower* achievement. The omission of a Same GPA comparison leaves open the possibility that a child with an IQ of 120 and a grade average of C may be no different educationally or psychologically than a child with an IQ of 100 and an identical grade average of C. If this were true, then one would argue that underachievement has no existence separate from low achievement.

Conclusion

These statistical and conceptual issues are real and valid, and they could produce intensive scholarly inquiry. But this is not our purpose in this book. Whether underachievement is error or whether the concept makes sense is assumed here to be an empirical question. Given the regression definition, we ask whether underachievement has systematic, interpretable relations with other variables. Are these relations unique to underachievers as opposed to those with the same grades? Error, by definition, is random, so if underachievement is error, few systematic relations should be found unless systematic bias is involved.

The task of science is to explain variance. A certain amount of variance in academic performance has historically been associated with mental ability, the remainder with other, potentially identifiable, sources. One source is random error. Other sources may represent bias, as in the case of different grading systems among schools or among subgroups within a sample whose average performance levels differ from one another.

Other sources may be more psychologically and educationally interesting, for example, rebelliousness and independence seeking in a student, a shy and nonassertive personality, an unmotivating educational system, a set of personal abilities and learning strategies that do not match the typical requirements of the classroom, low self-esteem, and so forth. We need to know if these factors are associated with underachievement in systematic and unique ways. Every teacher and school counselor, many family therapists, and some parents have seen youngsters who clearly are not achieving up to their potential and who seem to have unique attributes associated with their relatively poor performance. We believe underachievement exists. The task of scientifically charting its territory is more difficult than in many other domains, but it is the purpose of this book.

2

Who Is the Underachiever?

The inconsistencies of definition described in the previous chapter perhaps exert their greatest limitations on specifying some of the characteristics of underachievers. It is difficult, for example, to draw general conclusions across a literature varying so greatly in sample characteristics (e.g. gifted underachievers versus those that come from a broad spectrum of abilities), the definition of underachievement, and other parameters. It comes as no surprise that characteristics associated with underachievement (e.g., Socioeconomic Status [SES]) do not always replicate. But some characteristics can be discerned from this complicated literature.

Extent and Timing Parameters

FREQUENCY

As indicated above, because of the arbitrary extent to which performance deviates from predicted ability in the definition of underachievement, the percentage of students classified as underachievers will also be arbitrary. Therefore, the number or percentage of underachievers in a population cannot be specified in a meaningful way. For example, the most common and statistically appropriate definition of underachievers—students with negative deviations from the regression line greater than one standard error—will designate approximately 16% of the population of all students as underachievers (assuming a bivariate normal distribution of ability and performance measures). Because the regression procedure produces deviations from the regression line that are independent of mental ability, this percentage will be relatively constant across different ability levels (i.e., 16% of gifted students as well as of students of average ability would be designated as underachievers).

The situation becomes more complicated with other methods of defining underachievement. As mentioned above, a simple difference score produces a bias in which disproportionately more students of high ability and fewer of lower ability will be classified as underachievers, and the more extreme the ability score, the greater the bias. Similar biases are introduced by using the arbitrary absolute splits, but the consequences are less predictable. Using these methods, the percentage of gifted underachievers should be higher than the percentage of underachievers from other segments of the entire range of the ability dimension; and some studies have estimated the gifted underachievement rate to be as high as 50%, at least for males (see below).

AGE OF ONSET

It is reasonable for educators, psychologists, and parents to ask when underachievement typically emerges, but again the definition of underachievement does not permit this question to be answered directly. For example, pupils with a deviation greater than one standard error below the regression line of grades on mental ability can be labeled underachievers at any grade. There will always be underachievers by this method.

It is commonly reported that underachievement begins during the late elementary grades and certainly by junior high school, and that it begins earlier for boys (grade three) than for girls (grade nine). Where do these notions come from?

As early as 1960, Shaw and McCuen defined underachievers to be those students who scored in the top 25% of the eighth-grade school population on the Pinter General Ability Test: Verbal Series, but whose grade averages during grades 9, 10, and 11 were below the school average. A comparison group consisted of students with IQs in the upper 25% of the eighth-grade population whose high school grades were not below average. Then the investigators examined the school records and compared the achievers with the underachievers—defined during grades 8 to 11—on mean grade point average for each grade beginning with the first.

For males, high school underachievers had lower grade averages than the comparison group from the first grade onward, and the difference was significant by the third grade. The divergence continued to increase from grade to grade thereafter, primarily because of the continuing decline in the grade average for underachievers. The underachieving high school girls, however, were actually *better,* but not significantly so, than achievers in grade average through the fifth grade, at which point the underachievers began to decline, differing significantly by the ninth grade. This study has been interpreted as showing that male high school underachievers can be identified in early elementary school, but female high school underachievers are not distinguishable until junior high or early high school.

The age of onset of underachievement, then, is actually a question of the predictability or stability of underachievement, which depends on the age criterion, the definition of underachievement, and the method of assessing stability. For example, in one of the few longitudinal studies of underachievement, Kowitz and Armstrong (1961) calculated discrepancy scores separately at the third, sixth, and ninth grades. Relatively little consistency in who was an underachiever was observed from grade to grade, and patterns of underachievement seemed to be related to the particular academic subject involved as well as different school policies.

Whatever the technical issues may be, the assertion that underachievement begins in late elementary school nevertheless may be meaningful to educators, psychologists, and parents, if only because the problem becomes more noticeable to them at this time. Homework increases in late elementary and junior high school, for example, and students who refuse to complete homework or do it poorly are clearly identifiable. Some children, especially the gifted, may achieve easily and without effort through the first several grades, but give up when they meet the challenge of real production (homework) and mental effort, and are designated underachievers (Flowers, Horsman, & Schwartz, 1982).

The stability of underachievement raises another problem for definitions. The very fact that underachievers do not learn as much in school as would be expected will mean that their mental ability may decline to match their grades, at which point they will no longer be underachieving. Prolonged underachievement, then, may be unusual, not because of lack of stability in the psychological characteristics of such students, but because their mental ability has not been nurtured by effort in school.

Demographic Factors

SEX DIFFERENCES

A uniform finding in the literature is that underachievement is more characteristic of males than of females. Generally, two or three males are designated as underachievers for every female.

As early as 1963, Thorndike pointed out that any average difference in academic performance between boys and girls could influence the proportion of each sex classified as underachievers. If boys generally receive poorer grades than girls and if boys and girls are combined in one sample, then more boys than girls will be identified as underachievers. Relatively small differences between the sexes in average school performance can produce 2:1 ratios of male to female underachievers, and the smaller the percentage of students to be designated as underachievers, the smaller the difference between the means of the sexes necessary to produce large differences in the sex ratios of underachievers.

Assume that the 16% of students with the largest deviations below the regression line are denoted as underachievers with a sex ratio of two males to each female. This ratio would be produced if the difference in standard error between the males and the females is .365. Assuming a correlation of .65 between grades and mental ability and a standard error of .75 standardized grade units (see below), this sex ratio would be produced by a mean grade difference of .49 between the sexes. It is not unreasonable for the standard deviation of grades to be close to one, so an average sex difference of 0.5 grade point would produce a 2:1 ratio of male to female underachievers. Therefore, it is very likely that a substantial portion of the observed sex difference in the frequency of underachievement favoring males is a result of the generally lower average grades achieved by males relative to females.

But it would be glib and psychologically shortsighted to conclude that the 2+:1 male-to-female ratio of underachievers is nothing more than an artifact of the average difference in grades between males and females. Of course, one could define underachievers separately within sex, thereby arbitrarily producing equal numbers of males and females. But grades are not given separately for boys and girls, and no male student judges a poor report card to be "OK for a boy." Marathons may be scored separately for the sexes, but class rank is not. Even though the entire sex differential in underachievement may be associated with the sex difference in grade average, the students likely do not take that mean difference into account psychologically. And if girls generally have higher grade averages, in some sense it is reasonable that fewer girls should be underachievers. Therefore, the observation that underachievers consist of two or more males for every female is not "artifact" from a psychological perspective, but "explained" by the fact that males generally do more poorly in school.

PARENTAL EDUCATIONAL AND OCCUPATIONAL STATUS

It is often concluded in review articles (e.g., Dowdall & Colangelo, 1982; Pirozzo, 1982) that underachievers tend to have parents with relatively less education and lower occupational status than achievers. There is some evidence that this is true (e.g., Broman et al., 1985; Kurtz & Swenson, 1951; Musselman, 1942), but other studies show no differences (e.g., Goldberg, Bernhard, Kirschner, Hlavaty, Michelson, Goldberg, & Apel, 1959; Passow & Goldberg, 1963; Whitmore, 1980), and sometimes underachievers come from families with higher SES (Curry, 1961; Lowenstein, 1982).

This inconsistency may derive from differences in defining underachievement and the sample involved. Studies of gifted underachievers may find them to have well-educated parents, and children identified by teachers may have well-educated parents who contact teachers when their children do not perform up to expectations. Such children may display such commonly accepted signs of intelligence as verbal fluency in spite of their grades. In contrast, studies based on large samples representing a wide range of backgrounds and abilities tend to show underachievement to be associated with lower SES parents.

OTHER FACTORS

Many other demographic factors have been implicated, but the results are unclear.

Birth order. Although some have suggested that underachievers are typically later-born children with a high-achieving older sibling, little consistency exists in the literature regarding parity. Some investigators find underachievers to be predominantly firstborn (Newman, Dember, & Krug, 1973), others show no difference (Goldberg et al., 1959), and still others report they are more likely to be later-born children (Broman et al, 1985; Musselman, 1942).

Family size. A tendency exists for underachievers to come from larger families (Asbury, 1974; Broman et al., 1985; Musselman, 1942; Zilli, 1971), although Goldberg et al. (1959) reported no differences.

Size of town. A few studies suggest relatively more underachievers come from smaller towns than large cities (Flaugher & Rock, 1969; Musselman, 1942), but the data are fragmentary.

Working mothers. Although some data indicate higher percentages of working mothers among parents of underachievers (Kurtz & Swenson, 1951; Zilli, 1971), other investigators find no such relationship (Curry, 1961; Goldberg et al., 1959; Musselman, 1942; Passow & Goldberg, 1963).

Divorce. It is commonly asserted that underachievers are more likely to come from disrupted and single-parent households (Dowdall & Colangelo, 1982; Goldberg et al., 1959; Kurtz & Swenson, 1951; Passow & Goldberg, 1963; Zilli, 1971), although a few studies show no differences or even the opposite (e.g., Gowen, 1957; Musselman, 1942).

Although the data are not uniform, complete, or resting on the best methodology, underachievers tend to be disproportionately male (2:1 or 3:1) and from lower socioeconomic and larger families. Of course, these last two variables are correlated, and it may not be surprising, then, to find underachievers to be later-born children from larger families. Divorce is commonly reported to be more frequent in families of underachievers; this factor, too, may be associated with SES. Support for most of the characteristics discussed in this section depends on the nature of the sample and the definition of underachievement, again pointing to the need for a large and broadly based sample and defining underachievement across the entire range of ability.

Behavioral Characteristics of Underachievers and Their Parents

A variety of personal and psychological characteristics have been attributed to underachievers and their parents, based more on clinical impressions and reports of professionals, teachers, and parents than on systematic, objective measurements or observations. As mentioned above, no study has used a same-grades comparison group, so it is impossible to know whether such characteristics are unique to underachievement or are associated with low achievement in general. The variety of definitions of underachievers, sometimes involving only gifted students, further complicates interpretations. As several studies have recently reviewed this literature (e.g., Dowdall & Colangelo, 1982; Pirozzo, 1982; Whitmore, 1980, Zilli, 1971), it will be sketched here only in broad strokes.

CHARACTERISTICS OF UNDERACHIEVERS

Table 2.1 presents a listing, with sample references, of the major personality characteristics attributed to underachievers. Many of these attributes are illustrated by the case studies recounted in the prologue.

Self-perception. Generally, underachievers are believed to have a poor self-perception, poor self-concept, and low self-esteem, especially with regard to their academic abilities. They are often self-critical, fear both failure and success, and are anxious or nervous, especially over their performances.

Poor self-perception is one of the most commonly cited characteristics, although Davis and Connell (1985) claim that it is not a distinguishing feature. Barrett (1957) suggested that both underachievers and achievers suffer feelings of inadequacy, but where achievers are motivated to prove that they are indeed adequate, underachievers simply give up and withdraw from an achievement situation. The withdrawal is also seen as a sign of fear of failure or success, with youngsters feeling unable to risk a performance that might end in failure and so not trying at all. When success does come their way, underachievers may not know how to handle it. They may refrain from telling their parents for fear that the parents will continue to expect such performances, which the youngsters feel uncertain of reproducing.

Goal orientation. Underachievers are said to have faulty and unrealistic orientations toward goals. Specifically the standards they set for themselves are inappropriate, and gifted underachievers are often perfectionists, dissatisfied with every performance. Other underachievers have a complete lack of or very low educational and occupational aspirations. When presented with a task, they exhibit little persistence, especially in the face of challenge; and many react impulsively, dashing off any response and calling it done.

Peer relations. The vast majority of reports indicate that underachievers have very poor peer relationships. Typically they lack

TABLE 2.1 Personal characteristics of underachievers

Self-Perception
1. Low perception of abilities
   Bish (1963); Combs (1964); Durr & Collier (1960); Hoffman, Wasson, &
   Christianson (1985); Kurtz & Swenson (1951); Mallis (1983); Miller (1961);
   Pirozzo (1982); Richards, Gaver, & Golicz (1984); Rimm (1985a, 1985b);
   Trillingham & Bonsall (1963); Whitmore (1980); Zilli (1971).
2. Poor self-concept and low self-esteem
   Belcastro (1985); Bricklin & Bricklin (1967); Dowdall & Colangelo (1982); Fine
   & Pitts (1980); Fitzpatrick (1984); Hoffman et al. (1985); Jackson, Cleveland, &
   Merenda (1975); Lowenstein (1982); Mallis (1983); Miller (1961); Rimm
   (1985b); Rocks, Baker, & Guerney (1985); Taylor (1964); Teigland, Winkler,
   Munger, & Kranzler (1966); Whitmore (1980).
3. Self-critical
   Combs (1964); Fine (1967); Mallis (1983); Richards, Gaver, & Golicz (1984);
   Roth & Puri (1967).
4. Fear of failure, fear of success
   Bricklin & Bricklin (1967); Combs (1964); Heinemann (1977); Rimm (1985a,
   1985b); Sahler (1983).
5. Anxious, nervous (especially over performance)
   Bricklin & Bricklin (1967); Davis & Connell (1985); Durr & Collier (1960); Fine
   (1967); Hoffman et al. (1985); Richards et al. (1984); Taylor (1964).

Goal Orientation
6. Unrealistic standards; perfectionistic
   Clark (1979); Lowenstein (1982); Myers (1980); Richards et al. (1984); Rimm
   (1985a, 1985b); Taylor (1964); Westman & Bennett (1982); Whitmore (1980).
7. Lack of or low educational and occupational aspirations
   Bish (1963); Clark (1979); Fliegler (1957); Hummel & Sprinthall (1965); Kurtz &
   Swenson (1951); Myers (1980); Sahler (1983); Taylor (1964); Topol & Rexnikoff
   (1979); Zilli (1971).
8. Lack of persistence
   Belcastro (1985); Bricklin & Bricklin (1967); Combs (1964); Cutts & Moseley
   (1957); Fine (1967); Hoffman et al. (1985); McIntyre (1964); Rimm (1985a); Roth
   (1970); Shaw & McCuen (1960); Smart (1985); Taylor (1964).
9. Impulsive reaction to challenges
   Bish (1963); Fine (1967); Mallis (1983); Pecaut (1979).

Peer Relations
10. Lack of friends, lonely, alienated, withdrawn
    Barrett (1957); Belcastro (1985); Bish (1963); Davis & Connell (1985); Durr &
    Collier (1960); Fine & Pitts (1980); Goldberg et al. (1959); Gowan (1957); Hall
    (1983); Hoffman et al. (1985); Kurtz & Swenson (1951); McIntyre (1964); Pecaut
    (1979); Rimm (1984, 1985a); Roth (1970); Taylor (1964); Teigland et al. (1966);
    Whitmore (1980).

(Continued)

TABLE 2.1 (Continued)

11. Immature or ineffectual social skills, not liked by peers
Combs (1964); Dowdall & Colangelo (1982); Durr & Collier (1960); Hall (1983); Hummel & Sprinthall (1965); Jackson et al. (1975); Kurtz & Swenson (1951); Miller (1961); Newman, Dember, & Krug (1973); Rimm (1984); Teigland et al. (1966); Westman & Bennett (1985); Whitmore (1980).
12. Feel rejected
Combs (1964); Richards et al. (1984); Roth (1970); Taylor (1964); Whitmore (1980).

Authority Relationships
13. Overtly aggressive, hostile
Belcastro (1985); Fine (1967); Heinemann (1977); Mallis (1983); Miller (1961); Pecaut (1979); Pirozzo (1982); Rimm (1984, 1985a); Taylor (1964); Trillingham & Bonsall (1963); Whitmore (1980).
14. Discipline problems, delinquency
Dowdall & Colangelo (1982); Fine (1967); Fitzpatrick (1984); Gowan (1957); Greene (1963); Hoffman et al. (1985); Mallis (1983); Miller (1961); Pirozzo (1982); Rimm (1985a, 1985b); Rocks et al. (1985); Taylor (1964); Teigland et al. (1966).
15. Rebelliousness, independence striving
Combs (1964); Heinemann (1977); Hildreth (1966); Mallis (1983); Pecaut (1979); Rimm (1985b); Roth (1970); Sears & Sherman (1964); Taylor (1964); Whitmore (1980).
16. Lack of self-control, manipulative
Cutts & Moseley (1957); Hummel & Sprinthall (1965); Rimm (1985a, 1985b); Roth (1970).
17. Irresponsible, unreliable
Durr & Collier (1960); Hummel & Sprinthall (1965); Mallis (1983); Martin, Marx, & Martin (1980); McIntyre (1964); Rimm (1985b); Taylor (1964); Teigland et al. (1966); Trillingham & Bonsall (1963).
18. Passive-aggressive
Bricklin & Bricklin (1967); McIntyre (1964); Roth (1970).

Locus of Control
19. External control, blame others for problems or failure
Davis & Connell (1985); Hall (1983); Hoffman et al. (1985); McIntyre (1964); Miller (1961); Pecaut (1979); Rimm (1985b); Rocks et al. (1985); Roth (1970); Whitmore (1980); Zilli (1971).
20. Hypercritical of others, negativistic
Combs (1964); Fine (1967); Heinemann (1977); Mallis (1983); McIntyre (1964); Richards et al. (1984); Taylor (1964); Trillingham & Bonsall (1963); Zilli (1971).

Emotional Expression
21. Flat affect, apathy
Greene (1963); Martin et al. (1980); Taylor (1964).
22. Emotionally explosive, poorly controlled emotions
Combs (1964); Pecaut (1979).
23. Unhappy or depressed
Kurtz & Swenson (1951); Martin et al. (1980).

friends, and they are lonely and socially withdrawn. Such friends as they do have set little value on education and view school negatively (Kurtz & Swenson, 1951). Younger underachievers may be immature for their age or ineffectual in their social skills, disliked by their peers, and make friends younger than themselves. Some feel rejected.

Some authors suggest that a few underachievers are highly skilled socially, greatly involved in activities, and show good leadership abilities (Kurtz & Swenson, 1951; Rimm, 1984; Taylor, 1964). Some gifted underachievers are very sensitive to interpersonal relations, discriminating details in the personalities of other children and closely analyzing social behavior (Greene, 1963; Whitmore, 1980). Although some authors report that adolescent underachievers date less frequently (Roth, 1970), others indicate they date more and have more intense heterosexual relations (Rocks, Baker, & Guerney 1985) or have problems with heterosexual adjustment (Kurtz & Swenson, 1951).

Authority relations. Underachievers are often said to have problems relating to authority, initially their parents, then teachers, and finally other adults. They are overtly aggressive and hostile to authority figures, exhibit discipline problems and high rates of delinquency, lack self-control, and are irresponsible and unreliable. They also have serious problems establishing independence from their parents; they are often seen as rebellious and may be perceived as frequently attempting to manipulate others.

But some underachievers may express these aggressive tendencies more passively (Roth, 1970). Bricklin and Bricklin (1967) suggest that some underachievers hit their parents where it hurts the most—in the realm of achievement. McIntyre (1964) perceives the dawdling, stubborn, daydreaming, procrastinating, and obstructive underachiever as rebelling through inaction. Some will not be told to do anything, but cannot get tasks done on their own; others do what they are told up to a point, always doing it a bit differently as if to extract their pound of flesh for complying.

Locus of control. Generally, underachievers have an external locus of control. Some studies show this to be the case with respect to academic behaviors, but most report it in terms of blaming other people, rather than themselves, for problems or failures and of being hypercritical of others and negativistic toward them.

Emotional expression. Rarely are serious mental disturbances or even serious emotional problems mentioned. Occasionally, however, authors remark about underachievers' apathy and flat affect, sometimes describing them as unhappy or depressed. A few underachievers are said to be emotionally explosive and poorly controlled.

Types of underachievers. Underachievers represent a particular segment of the individual difference dimension defined by the discrepancy between grades and some measure of ability. Scholars have suggested further individual differences within the underachievement category, describing different types or syndromes of underachievers on the basis of their behaviors and presumed dynamics. Clearly, some of the attributes listed here are correlated, but others are mutually incompatible and must characterize different individuals (e.g., shy/withdrawn versus aggressive).

Roth (1970) distinguished three types of underachievers (see also later section, "Theories and Prognosis"). One is the *neurotic underachiever* preoccupied with his or her relationship with parents and suffering from substantial anxiety and guilt over it. The second exhibits the *nonachievement syndrome,* choosing to make no effort and therefore failing. The third type is characterized by *adolescent reaction,* consisting of extreme independence seeking and attempting to do everything parents oppose.

Pecaut (1979) outlined four types. *Trust seekers* are lonely, isolated, withdrawn, impulsive, and emotionally explosive. *Approval seekers* are indecisive; they try to fulfill the expectations of others, but may stop attempting to do so, have serious test anxiety, need praise, and are afraid of authority. *Dependency seekers* are selectively uninterested in certain basic subjects in elementary school, ambivalent to authority, passive-aggressive, and socially gregarious. They project responsibility onto others for their failures. A final group, *independence seekers,* feel conflict about independence and dependence from parents, value whatever is opposite to that emphasized by parents and other adults, and are hostile and rebellious toward adult authority.

In one of the more comprehensive recent analyses, Whitmore (1980) distinguished three types similar to those noted by Roth (1970) and Taylor (1990). She suggested that three out of four underachievers are *aggressive*—disruptive, talkative, clowning in class, rebellious, and hostile. In contrast, the *withdrawn* underachievers are uninterested, bored, and do not try or participate. The third type is a *combination* of the aggressive and withdrawn, erratic, unpredictable, and vacillating between aggression and withdrawal. Their work habits are inconsistent, sometimes good and sometimes poor, and they are often seen as lazy or immature. They may have many friends, but they can be aggressive or withdrawn. Whitmore's scheme seems simple, empirical, and most congruent with the results of other studies.

PARENTAL CHARACTERISTICS

Parents of underachievers have been described generally as being either indifferent or overly preoccupied with their child's achievement. General parental characteristics are outlined in Table 2.2.

Indifference. Perhaps the most commonly described characteristics of parents of underachievers include indifference, lack of interest, distant relationships with minimum affection, and neutral to negative attitudes toward education. These characteristics may occur singly or in combination with two other themes. One is an authoritarian, restrictive, and rejecting style, especially by the father. The second involves extreme permissiveness and freedom, bordering on neglect in some homes. With a gifted underachiever, it may be more a case of the child leading the parent, who treats the child as an independent, miniature adult.

Overemphasis on achievement. Parents' high valuation of achievement plus clear expectations about performance are typically correlates of high achievement in offspring, but too much parental pressure, pushiness, and preoccupation with achievement to the

TABLE 2.2 Parental characteristics of underachievers

Indifferent, Uninterested, Distant, Low Affection; Neutral to Negative Attitudes Toward Education

Barrett (1957); Drews & Teahan (1957); Fliegler (1957); Gowan (1957); Gurman (1970); Khatena (1982); Kurtz & Swenson (1951); Miller (1961); Pirozzo (1982); Rocks et al. (1985); Sears & Sherman (1964); Strang (1951); Taylor (1964); Westman & Bennett (1985).

1. Authoritarian, restrictive, rejecting

Fliegler (1957); Khatena (1982); McIntyre (1964); Pirozzo (1982); Roth (1970); Taylor (1964); Westman & Bennett (1985); Zilli (1971).

2. Extreme permissiveness and freedom; "adultizing" (especially of gifted children)

Gurman (1970); Lowenstein (1982); McIntyre (1964); Rimm (1984); Zilli (1971).

Overemphasis on Achievement

1. Too much pressure, preoccupation with achievement

Bricklin & Bricklin (1967); Gurman (1970); Lowenstein (1982); McIntyre (1964); Miller (1961); Roth (1970); Strang (1951); Zilli (1971).

2. Overindulgent, oversolicitous, overprotective, too helpful

Barrett (1957); Fliegler (1957); Khatena (1982); McIntyre (1964); Pirozzo (1982); Rimm (1984); Roth (1970); Westman & Bennett (1985).

Parental Disagreement, Conflict, Inconsistency

Fliegler (1957); Holmes (1962); McIntyre (1964); Pless & Satterwhite (1973); Rimm (1984); Roth (1970); Taylor (1964); Westman & Bennett (1985); Zilli (1971); Zuccone & Amerikaner (1986).

exclusion of all other characteristics of the child can lead to under-achievement.

Another common theme is the overindulgent, oversolicitous, over-protective parent who is simply too helpful. The parent reminds, teaches, and helps the child accomplish every task. In the early years, the child is rewarded for seeking help because the well-intended parent dispenses it eagerly. But the result can be that the child comes to believe that he or she cannot do anything independently and fails to develop responsibility, self-sufficiency, or feelings of self-fulfillment.

Parental inconsistency. The situation may be even worse if the two parents represent different styles. Rimm (1984) describes at least three types of families. In one, father is an ogre—restrictive, authoritarian, and controlling—but mother capitulates to the child, trying to compensate. The opposite situation occurs when mother is an ogre (also described by McIntyre, 1964). A third type of inconsistency occurs when father is a "dummy," and mother feels she knows how to rear the children. Perhaps she has a college education and courses in education and psychology, but her husband is uneducated or simply withdraws from childrearing in the face of her dominance. In each of these cases, there is a strong and a weak parent, neither of which may promote achievement; and the combination allows the child to play one parent off against the other.

School Behaviors and Environment

Ironically, although underachievement is defined in terms of school performance, relatively little empirical attention has been paid to systematically studying the school behavior of these children. Indirectly, then, less blame seems to be placed on schools than on the children or their parents.

Table 2.3 lists school behaviors of underachievers that are frequently mentioned in the literature. Although some are based on systematic data collection (e.g., Fine, 1967; Whitmore, 1980), most are casual descriptions derived from the experience of teachers or counselors.

Few scholars argue directly that underachievers are poorly served by the schools. When this assertion is made, it usually refers to gifted underachievers, who are sometimes thought to be bored or unstimulated in school (Mallis, 1983; Pirozzo, 1982; Sahler, 1983). Torrance (1962) and Whitmore (1980) comment on the gifted child's creativity in particular, which may not fit the typical classroom situation, which focuses on one right answer. Whitmore (1980) and Myers (1980) argue that regular teachers, curricula, and the typical classroom climate are unsuitable for gifted children. Teachers may judge students only on the basis of their performance (Stern, 1963); apply unreasonable pressure for achievement (Lowenstein, 1982); and conduct strict, repressive, autocratic classes emphasizing rote and repetitive learning (Pirozzo, 1982) inappropriate for gifted students.

TABLE 2.3 School behaviors of underachievers

Discipline
> Tardy, absent
> Disruptive, talkative, discipline problem
> Immature, maladjusted

Work Habits
> Poor study skills, deficient in basic skills and problem solving
> Inconsistent effort and quality of performance
> Lack of concentration, daydreaming, hyperactive, restless
> Disorganized, distractible
> Sloppy, impulsive work; does just enough to get by
> Does not try, fails to do homework
> Runs away from challenges, problems

School Attitude
> Bored, disinterested, does not participate
> Hates school
> Indifferent to failure

Interpersonal
> Openly resentful, hostile, aggressive
> Seeks attention
> Cries easily
> Shy, withdrawn

Low SES and Minority Underachievers

The bulk of the literature focuses on gifted underachievers who typically come from the upper-middle classes. Myers (1980) suggests special factors may be involved for underachieving children from lower socioeconomic classes. Such children often attend poor quality schools, teachers do not expect very much of them and may not recognize the abilities they possess, and their families may have low expectations and limited resources to support academic achievement.

Similarly, underachievers from cultural minorities also may lack parents or teachers who expect achievement, who encourage it, and who are able to support it. In some groups, achievement is seen as sissified for boys, and cultural norms emphasize street smarts, athletics, and survival skills rather than academic knowledge.

Teachers may refuse to take a high test score as a serious sign of ability when it is produced by a student who does not look or act like most academically achieving students. An upper-middle-class student with an ability-performance discrepancy may be viewed as performing poorly, but a lower class or minority student as merely testing well, a situation calling for no special attention or even considered a fluke.

Theories

Perhaps the only agreement among those who have tried to theorize about underachievement is that it is caused by several factors, which may operate alone, in small sets, or in complex interaction.

PARTICULAR THEORIES

Krouse and Krouse. Krouse and Krouse (1981) suggested that conceptual models of underachievement can be grouped into four categories:

1. skills deficiency, especially in basic areas such as reading and mathematics
2. personality dysfunction
3. deficits in self-control
4. interfering anxiety

Krouse and Krouse (1981) proposed that the academic, self-control, and affective forces often interact with one another. A student who is poor in reading can develop a negative self-concept and low self-esteem, which the student then attempts to avoid facing by failing to study and seeking distractions and diversions. This lack of self-control produces further decrements in the student's academic performance, and the cycle continues.

Pecaut. Some theorists concentrate on one or two of these factors, especially the child's personality; Pecaut (1979), whose ideas have been discussed above, emphasizes personality above other factors, suggesting that underachievers seek either trust, approval, dependency, or independence. Westman and Bennett (1985) believe that underachievers wish to remain young children and do not want to grow up, much like Peter Pan, and so are more motivated to fail than to succeed.

Whitmore. Whitmore (1980) applies Thibaut and Kelly's (1959) theory of the comparison level for alternatives (Jones & Gerard, 1967) to the case of underachievers. Basically, the theory postulates that individuals pursue activities that are rewarding to them and avoid ones that are not. Presumably, the underachiever has found academic tasks and activities unrewarding and so seeks rewards elsewhere. The child may become socially active, the class clown, or an athlete. If rewards are not derived from peers in these contexts, the child may withdraw or become aggressively dominating in an effort to reap the needed rewards. As total avoidance of school is not possible, children develop a variety of strategies for coping with the compulsory relationships with the teacher and school. Some devalue school and the teacher ("Who cares, anyway?"); some avoid participation as much as possible; some comply, but with chronic complaint; others comply, but find compensatory relief in disrupting class or performing assignments in unique ways; and still others project blame for their failures on other people. Some simply emphasize more rewarding activities, and others displace their hostility on other people and circumstances. Basically then, inactivity or disruptive behavior can be viewed as compensation for feelings of low self-esteem and as manifestations of frustration combined with the fear of failure.

Developmental Theory Model. The oldest and most comprehensive theory is the Developmental Theory Model (Roth, Berenbaum, & Hershenson, 1967), which Mandel and Marcus (1988) recently summarized. Following standard psychiatric diagnoses (i.e., DSM-III), the Developmental Theory Model asserts that underachievement is a result of fixation in development, and underachievers have different characteristics depending upon the stage at which fixation occurs.

Five categories of underachievers are proposed, including, with DSM-III references, the Overanxious Disorder (313.00), the Conduct Disorder (312.00, 312.20, 312.90), the Academic Problem or Non-Achievement Syndrome (V62.30), the Identity Disorder (313.82), and the Oppositional Defiant Disorder (313.81).

Mandel and Marcus (1988) reviewed the literature on the Developmental Theory Model and argue that these types of disorders can be reliably and differentially diagnosed, that nonachievement and other symptoms differ as a function of these categories, and that observable symptomatology corresponds with that specified in DSM-III. The empirical literature varies in the strength of support it confers on these assertions. Although the Developmental Theory Model has generated the most research, no theory has been comprehensively studied with appropriate comparison groups and no objective instruments have been designed expressly for the purpose of testing a theory or validating the existence of different types of underachievers as postulated by these theories. Much empirical work remains to be done in this regard.

Metacognitive Motivational Model. Borkowski, Carr, Rellinger, and Pressley, (1990) emphasize motivational and metacognitive differences between underachievers and achieving students. Underachievers appear to have learned to be helpless—they do not believe that their knowledge, skills, and experiences are the product of their own abilities and efforts—they are externally controlled. Success, when it occurs, is not a product of their efforts, but of uncontrollable external factors, such as luck. They see no need to try or work hard, and resulting failures lower their self-esteem and further reduce their motivation.

The characteristics described by this approach are frequently attributed to underachievers (witness the review above). Indeed, these characteristics are almost synonymous with the clinical syndrome of underachievement. But, as in nearly all the literature summarized here, it is not clear that these characteristics apply to underachievers as distinct from low achievers with the same grades but less ability (e.g., Carr, Borkowski, & Maxwell, 1991).

Theoretical work on underachievement is not well developed. Some theories are not tied to specific measures and therefore difficult to test, and others have not been tested against Same GPA comparison groups.

3

Prognosis and
Treatment

Not surprising, given the diversity of views regarding the major characteristics of underachievers and the dynamics producing the syndrome, approaches to prognosis and treatment have been diverse and the literature on their effectiveness is checkered.

Prognosis

If left untreated, what is the prognosis for underachievers? No one knows, because underachievers rarely have been systematically studied in a longitudinal manner, even during their school years and certainly not thereafter.

Speculations on the long-term prognosis depend on the discipline of the speculator. Clinicians, who believe the underlying problem, whatever its initial causes, resides within the child, tend to believe underachievement will persist without treatment. Indeed, the literature on treatment outcomes reveals a somewhat bleak outlook (see below), suggesting that underachievement is sufficiently persistent that it even resists many attempts at treatment.

Those who believe school performance plays a formative role in the educational and occupational lives of Americans also believe in the persistence of underachievement. They are supported by longitudinal studies of large samples of representative youth (not specifically underachievers) showing that education is the major determinant of later occupational status, even mediating the contribution of ability and social status (e.g., Alexander & Eckland, 1975; Blau & Duncan, 1967; Duncan, 1961; Sewell, Haller, & Ohlendorf, 1970; Sewell, Haller, & Portes, 1969; Sewell & Hauser, 1972).

School counselors sometimes take another view. Parents who complain to school personnel are often told that their underachieving child will grow out of the problem, especially once the youth leaves home, goes to college, or must make it on his or her own. And parents sometimes report that such youth eventually do "get their acts together," although often only after several years as a "couch potato." Clinicians tend to see the most severe cases and remain skeptical that such underachievers will recover without treatment; some privately suggest that treatment must be started early if it is to have much chance of correcting the problem.

These speculations sound contradictory, but they all could be true. As a total group, untreated underachievers may not attain adult educational and occupational status consistent with their tested abilities, but undoubtedly a few individuals do attain these levels. Although some eventually go to college and do reasonably well occupationally, on average they may not attain the high levels of achievement that would have been predicted on the basis of their abilities. In subsequent chapters, we will attempt to address these issues.

Intervention and Treatment

The literature on treatment approaches and their effectiveness has undergone progressive changes through the years, but generally falls into two epochs.

EARLY STUDIES

Four reviews of research done prior to approximately 1980 agreed that beneficial consequences of intervention and treatment were modest at best, and no single approach could claim consistent results (Dowdall & Colangelo, 1982; Krouse & Krouse, 1981; Pirozzo, 1982; Whitmore, 1980).

Krouse and Krouse (1981) categorized intervention and treatments into four groups:

1. Academic remediation with an emphasis on study skills (e.g., the "SQ3R" method) and remediation for specific skill deficits. Results mixed.
2. Psychotherapy. Results inconsistent.
3. Promoting self-control through self-monitoring, self-reinforcement, and stimulus control. Results mixed.
4. Reducing interfering anxiety (e.g., test anxiety). Test anxiety invariably reduced, but concurrent improvement in academic performance not always observed.

Pirozzo (1982) saw the remediation literature representing two major strategies (most programs are actually a mixture of both):

1. Personal counseling, especially to combat low self-image and feelings of inferiority. Evidence of effectiveness neither consistent nor conclusive, but the counseling employed in many studies was limited in scope and lasted for only short periods of time.
2. Changes in the educational environment and programming. Typically homogeneous grouping or special classes for underachievers, but ability grouping by itself does not necessarily produce greater academic achievement.

Dowdall and Colangelo (1982) also grouped interventions into counseling versus manipulating the classroom environment and drew the same conclusions as Pirozzo (1982). In addition, they suggest that classroom modifications, often not initiated until high school, might be more beneficial if started earlier.

Although overall the literature is inconsistent, a few studies are important for the influence they have exerted on the field or for their methodological characteristics.

Goldberg et al. (1959), in a very early study, created a special, relatively unstructured, social studies class for one hour each day for gifted underachieving boys, in which the teacher developed a close relationship with the students, who were encouraged and rewarded for any initiative and success. At the end of the first semester, the teacher felt the boys had benefited greatly from the experience, but their grades in other classes had not improved. The special students increased their participation in school activities, however—as they were encouraged to do—more than controls. By the end of the academic year, their grades improved in all subjects except the special class; grades declined for the control group.

Homogeneous grouping was expanded from one hour to the entire school day by Karnes, McCoy, Zehrbach, Wollersheim, and Clarizio (1963). Twenty-five gifted underachievers in one school were placed in a homogeneous classroom containing gifted achievers while 23 gifted underachievers in another school were randomly interspersed among the several heterogeneous classes at their grade level. To focus the interpretive emphasis on homogeneous versus heterogeneous grouping, instructional materials and services were made available equally to both schools. The homogeneous group made greater gains in academic achievement, had a higher level of ability on the fluency factor of creativity, and gained in perceived positive parental attitudes. This study is frequently cited as the rationale for homogeneous classrooms. Unfortunately, a single homogeneous classroom was compared with several heterogeneous classes, thereby confounding schools and teacher with the main manipulation and introducing the possibility of a halo effect.

Perkins and Wicas (1971) gave 12 weekly, one-hour group counseling sessions to either six junior high underachieving boys, six underachieving boys and their mothers in separate sessions, or only the mothers of six underachieving boys. These groups were compared to a no-treatment control group. Grades improved for all of the counseled groups relative to the controls, with no differences among the three treatment groups. But an interpersonal checklist rating self-acceptance showed improvement only among treatment groups in which mothers were counseled. No differences occurred with respect to study habits, anxiety, or school absences. Although other studies of counseling have yielded mixed results, this study showed some advantage to counseling parents over simply counseling the students.

Directing treatment at parents and teachers of underachievers in the fourth, fifth, and sixth grades was emphasized by Jackson, Cleveland, and Merenda (1975). Sessions centered on the child's potential capabilities and assets, improving self-esteem, and constructing appropriate learning situations for the child. One of the few longitudinal follow-ups of any intervention program showed the treatment group, relative to uncounseled students, attaining higher rank in class near the end of high school and higher scores on an achievement test and on the ACT College Entrance Test, with nonsignificant tendencies to plan more for further education and to hold higher educational expectations. In a telephone or letter follow-up 6 months after high school graduation, more of the counseled underachievers had actually gone on to some form of a higher education (75% versus 54%), and a greater percentage of the counseled students actually did what they had planned before leaving high school. One year after high school graduation, there was no difference in college dropout rates among those who attended college. The Jackson et al. and Perkins and Wicas studies both emphasized involving parents in the intervention, and the Jackson et al. project represents one of the few documented improvements assessed several years after the intervention.

RECENT INTERVENTIONS

More recent attempts to treat underachievers have taken different forms with somewhat more consistent positive results of at least a modest magnitude, although the descriptions of some programs and results are very sketchy.

Social skills training. Two programs emphasized training to improve social skills and social relationships, with resulting improvement in certain aspects of social and classroom behavior, but a less profound impact on achievement.

Rotheram (1982) provided social skills training to underachieving students and to disruptive and exceptional children in the fourth, fifth, and sixth grades and compared them with no-treatment controls. The training consisted of a drama simulation game played for one hour twice a week for 12 weeks that taught assertiveness, solving social problems, group problem solving, and behavioral rehearsal and feedback on performance. The trained students reported more social assertiveness, peers rated them as being more popular within the social skills classes, and teachers rated them higher on achievement and classroom comportment than controls both immediately and one year following the intervention.

Rocks, Baker, and Guerney (1985) investigated the effectiveness of a modified version of Guerney's (1977) Relationship Enhancement Program, which is aimed at improving interpersonal communications and awareness of one's feelings, perceptions, and desires. The program was administered either to both teachers and students or just to teachers, and in two forms, either the complete Relationship Enhancement training or a brief lecture/discussion session about open and good communications. Classroom behavior was reported to improve in pre-post comparisons when both teachers and students were given the full program, but no change was found in academic achievement, attendance, or school attitudes. Thus, some improvement in social relations and classroom behavior may be produced by direct training in these areas, but the effect of such intervention on academic performance remains unclear.

Study and academic skills. Other investigators have emphasized training in study and other academic skills together with activities designed to improve self-esteem. Improvements in the areas trained have been found with some consistency, but the effects on general academic performance are inconsistent.

Crittenden, Kaplan, and Heim (1984) gave seven weekly, 2-hour sessions to 16 underachieving children in the sixth through the ninth grades at the Reading and Language Development Clinic at the University of California Medical Center, San Francisco. Training was in study methods (e.g., SQ3R), report writing, creative written expression, time and behavior management, and realistic self-appraisal and self-confidence. Participants improved more than nonparticipants in self-concept, written language, and study skills, but not in areas that were not specifically taught.

Markle, Rinn, and Goodwin (1980) gave 21 males and 6 females who were 9 to 17 years of age an Achievement Motivation Training program conducted in five sessions each lasting approximately 75 minutes; achievement motivation was discussed; homework was assigned and discussed; guidance on classroom behavior, study habits, and test taking was provided; and realistic goals were encouraged. Relative to a no-treatment control group as well as a within-treatment matched control group, grades did improve (2.30 versus 1.85 pre-post) for the counseled subjects.

Fitzpatrick (1984) provided underachievers of average intellectual ability in the ninth grade with the Secondary III Core Program, which emphasizes training study skills and improving self-concept. Self-concept, grades, and attitudes toward school improved as measured before and after treatment as well as in follow-ups at 6 months and 1 year after the program.

Gerler (Gerler, Kinney, & Anderson, 1985; Gerler, Bland, Melang, & Miller, 1986) studied individual and group interventions that emphasized study skills, school attitudes, self-esteem, and emotional expression as well as interpersonal behaviors. The program was given by school counselors to third- and fourth-grade underachievers who were compared pre-post as well as with a no-treatment control group. Some behavioral contracting and reinforcements for appropriate behaviors were also administered. The counseled students improved significantly on the self-rating scale of classroom behavior as well as in their mathematics and language arts grades, but teachers did not share the perception of improvement in classroom behavior. In a second report (Gerler et al., 1986), the results on classroom behavior ratings were the opposite—the teachers (who knew which students participated in the intervention) perceived classroom behavior to improve, but the students themselves did not share this perception.

Apparently, some improvement in academic performance may derive from group tutoring in study skills, homework, and attempts to improve self-concept, although the effects do not seem large and one does not know if performance reached levels expected on the basis of the student's ability.

Comprehensive programs. Two studies report attempts to involve students, parents, and teachers in comprehensive programs that produced some improvement in grades. McGuire and Lyons (1985) tried a "transcontextual" model of family therapy with 17 families who had been referred to the community mental health center of a midwestern metropolitan hospital for treatment of an underachieving child. Treatments started with family therapy, followed by family-school sessions involving a version of the periodic progress report system (see below). Thirteen of 16 underachievers who were available for follow-up 6 months after treatment had improved their grade averages, 7 by more than one grade.

Lowenstein (1982) administered 6 months of treatment in which parents were encouraged to increase their interest in their underachieving child and provide some academic tutoring, teachers were instructed to establish a warm relationship with the student and to construct a system of reinforcements for a student's success, and a psychologist was to diagnose and follow up on emotional problems. The subjects were 9 to 18 years of age. Compared to a no-treatment control group, the treated underachievers gained in reading and spelling, but not in mathematics performance.

A small study on peer tutoring was reported by Kehayan (1983), involving seventh and eighth grade students with motivational and attitudinal problems and some history of behavioral delinquency. Their IQs were average or above average. They were exposed to the Peer Intervention Network, an organized peer tutoring and support group, combined with a version of the periodic progress report system. Over a 3-year period (approximately eight students per year), Kehayan reports that grade averages improved from 1.0 to 2.0.

Finally, Whitmore (1980) provides one of the most comprehensive reviews of research on gifted underachievers and one of the most detailed descriptions of an intervention in the literature. Whitmore argues that counseling of children and/or parents as well as skill training will never be more than partly successful with gifted under-achievers unless the classroom milieu is adjusted to accommodate the gifted child's special needs.

A special classroom was established in the Cupertino (California) schools for underachieving gifted children in the second grade—one of the earliest interventions reported in the literature. The goals of the special class were to enable more frequent social and academic success, promote self-governing behaviors, increase the emotional adjustment and maturity of the child, enhance self-concept and self-esteem, accelerate the socialization of the child, reduce the gap between aptitude and academic achievement, and improve perfor-mance to a level one year above chronological grade in most subjects.

These goals were to be accomplished by emphasizing competi-tion, providing an atmosphere of cooperation and individual self-evaluation toward personal goals, developing self-acceptance through accepting others with similar problems, providing a curricu-lum that centered on the child's individual strengths and areas of past successes, concentrating on genuine success experiences, and devel-oping social and leadership skills. The program was distinct from, but labeled as part of, the district program for gifted students, rather than identified as a program for handicapped or poorly performing stu-dents. The classroom atmosphere maximized individual work and flexibility in a student-centered and individually tailored program. Parents attended twice-monthly meetings to evaluate the child's progress and to receive information about gifted underachievers, the curriculum, and improving relations at home.

Whitmore (1980) reported results for a total of 29 students who were in the program from 1 to 3 years between 1968 and 1971 and who were assessed at various points during the next few years. Comparisons were mainly pre-post. According to teachers', parents', and students' anecdotal and evaluation records and some objective instruments, students became much more interested in school. They improved in decision making and self-direction; set more realistic goals and self-evaluations; underwent fewer incidents of frustration, anxiety, or expressions of self-contempt; achieved higher levels of cooperative social interaction; and improved their relationships with parents and siblings. The students rated themselves as declining over the treatment period in convergent mental ability and work habits, but increasing in school competency, results that were interpreted to reflect a more realistic self-concept and individual adoption of higher standards as a result of the special classroom.

In addition, the students' locus of control became more internal for both successes and failures, and academic achievement improved. At the end of the first year of the program, only 3 of 18 students remained below grade level on standardized tests in reading or math, and 12 showed a gain of at least 1.5 years in reading. Similar results occurred in subsequent years, and these gains were made in a program that did not focus on direct tuition in basic skills.

Whitmore conducted follow-up studies 1 to 3 years later in which 9 to 16 of the original 29 treated subjects were compared with students in grades three to six who had been recommended for placement, but not enrolled. Teachers reported better behavior and attitudes at school for the treated students, but no difference in work habits and social adjustment. The treated students reported a better self-concept, but parents reported no differences between the groups.

The results were less encouraging in a similar follow-up of nine junior high boys who had been in the special class. These program graduates held very negative attitudes toward school, perhaps because they rebelled against the schools they subsequently attended, and they also perceived that adults did not accept and respect them as individuals. Six of the nine had low self-concepts, which may also have been associated with their school environment.

A few years later, a mailed follow-up survey found teachers still positive about the classroom behavior of treated students, but the students continued to hold negative attitudes toward school. There was some tendency for students to lose more ground if they left special classes for the gifted than if they remained in them.

Generally, the study shows the potential of specialized classes for gifted underachievers in improving classroom behavior and performance, self-esteem, and attitudes toward school, benefits which can be maintained to some extent if these gifted underachievers are "grad-uated" to special classes for gifted achieving students rather than returned to regular classrooms.

The Periodic Progress Report System. Although not studied in the context of underachievement per se, the Periodic Progress Report System (PPRS) has been used to change the same school behaviors that characterize underachievers. PPRS is simply a daily or weekly report card covering the behaviors to be encouraged (e.g., completes homework satisfactorily, acceptable classroom behavior) that is completed by each teacher, brought to a counselor, and then sent home, where the parent dispenses rewards for appropriate behavior and progress.

Atkeson and Forehand (1978, 1979), after reviewing the research evidence, concluded that the PPRS can effectively change a variety of academic and deportment behaviors in students across a wide age range, and that although praise is useful, it is generally not a suffi-ciently powerful reinforcement unless accompanied by privileges or material rewards. In the context of underachievement, the PPRS may be especially well suited to encourage the shy youngster who needs extra rewards for appropriate behavior and make the rebellious stu-dent responsible for his or her actions. Few data are available on the use of the PPRS to change other aspects of underachievement or on the longer-term outcomes of its use as the primary remedial approach.

Conclusion. Although overall the research results are inconsistent, a tendency does exist toward gains primarily in areas emphasized by the particular intervention strategy. It appears that real success expe-riences, perhaps promoted through the use of the periodic progress report system, do improve self-concept and performance, and social skill training, remedial academic skills training, education and train-ing of parents, some personal counseling of students, and specialized classrooms (especially for gifted underachievers) each can contribute to a comprehensive treatment program.

Regrettably, the commonly used treatment approaches of tutoring (e.g., privately, in national chains) and private therapy have not been publicly evaluated, and no information is available about their effectiveness. Nor have there been evaluations of the programs used by the few schools or school systems who at least try to identify and help pupils who are underachievers, but have no other identifiable problem.

4

Background of the
Current Study

The literature reviewed in the previous chapters reveals several problems and gaps in our knowledge of underachievers. In addition to inconsistencies in the operational definition of underachievers, most studies have been based on small samples representing only a narrow range of abilities; used only a few objective measures to describe the personal and social characteristics of underachievers; lacked comparison groups, especially students having the same grades as underachievers; and omitted long-term follow-ups to determine what happens to underachievers after leaving school. Our study is unique in its attempt to fill this void.

Purpose

Our study had a very practical purpose. The major questions of our research were:

1. Is there a syndrome of underachievement—a set of characteristics unique in nature or degree to underachievers that separates them from pupils with either the same grades or the same mental ability who are not underachieving?

The literature has generally lacked any comparison of underachievers with same-grade controls. As a result, it really is not known if underachievers are any different from low-achieving pupils who are getting grades consistent with their mental ability. In short, is underachievement a psychologically meaningful syndrome? We approached this question empirically, not conceptually, by searching for attributes that distinguished underachievers from comparison groups of students with the same grade point averages.

2. What happens educationally, occupationally, and maritally to underachievers 13 years after high school?

Essentially, no study of untreated underachievers has looked at the consequences of underachievement per se several years after high school. Do these youths eventually achieve educationally and occupationally at a level that would be predicted on the basis of their ability, as counselors sometimes assure parents? Or do they only achieve the levels that might be expected from their grades, presumably wasting some of their mental ability? The question is important because few schools, school systems, or states routinely or systematically search for and provide special assistance to underachievers unless they have some other characteristic (e.g., learning disability, emotional disturbance) that qualifies them for special programming.

Note that this is a study of characteristics and outcome, not process or causes. It is intensely empirical and practical, not theoretical or conceptual. It is oriented toward the clinical and counseling concerns of education and psychology, not the scholarly interests of psychometrics or sociology. And the methods are correspondingly practical and applied. We could have done otherwise and still found our work useful and important. The questions, methods, and statistics would have been different—valid for these other purposes, but different. Our justification for the particular statistical approach we follow in this book will appear later in this chapter after the methods are presented.

UNIQUE FEATURES

The present study had several unique features.

Number of underachievers and ability levels. Much past study is based on small samples—perhaps a single special classroom or students in a single school identified by a counselor as underachievers. The emphasis has been on gifted underachievers, but students of other ability levels may also underachieve. To the best of our knowledge, our study covers the largest sample of underachieving boys and girls with the largest range of ability levels in the literature. Data from this study will balance many previous studies in which the correlates of underachievement may reflect the narrowness of their samples.

School ages. We defined underachievers primarily in their junior year in high school, although most earlier investigations focused on younger underachievers. Consequently, interpretations must emphasize the fact that underachievers in this study had shown persistent underachievement during their high school careers (their grade average for all of high school was included in defining underachievement) and their underachievement was displayed late in adolescence (if not also earlier). Because those students who dropped out of high school earlier than approximately their junior year were not included in the study—less than 1% of the current sample failed to complete high school— the sample does not include the most serious underachievers, the dropouts.

No special services. It is unlikely that the current students received many special services stimulated by their underachievement, because the sample was enrolled in high school during the early and mid-1960s when special and remedial services for students with learning or achievement problems were not nearly as prevalent as they are today. However, no data were available on the presence of such services or which subjects might have received them. The sample could include students who performed poorly because of physical and neurological disorders rather than simple lack of motivation, although they would have had to score better on the ability measure than their performance indicated to qualify as underachievers.

Extensive data set. The individuals in this sample responded to an extensive questionnaire regarding their educational and occupational behaviors, aspirations, and expectations; their self-concept; peer relations; relations with parents; and a variety of demographic indices. This is probably the broadest, most systematically collected, contemporary data set on underachievers in the literature.

Correlates and syndromes. The extensive contemporaneous data permitted a systematic study of the correlates of underachievement and the exploration of syndromes of underachievement. Some underachievers may be rebelling against their parents, others are shy and withdrawn, and still others are too busily engaged in extracurricular activities to study up to their potential. The current data permitted an empirical examination of such types and syndromes.

Comparison groups. Comparison groups were constructed and matched with the underachievers to control for grades or for mental ability. This design permitted us to address the question of whether the correlates of underachievement were simply correlates of grades, correlates of their mental ability, or correlates unique to underachievers. Such a comparison had not been carried out previously.

Long-term follow-up. A unique feature of these data is that 98.2% of the entire original sample from which the underachievers were drawn were located and assessed 13 years after high school graduation with respect to certain aspects of their lives and their educational and occupational histories and achievements. No study of underachievers per se, treated or untreated, has followed them over this long a period of time.

SPECIFIC QUESTIONS

The specific questions addressed in this extensive data set included:

1. Is underachievement distinguishable from low grades in terms of contemporary correlates and later educational and occupational attainments?

2. Do the correlates of underachievement based upon limited and often specialized samples replicate on a large sample of underachievers spanning the entire range of ability levels?
3. Are there syndromes or types of underachievement that can be discerned empirically by clustering underachievers on the basis of variables thought to be related to achievement in general and underachievement in particular?
4. Do untreated underachievers attain levels of educational and occupational status 13 years after high school that are consistent with what would be predicted on the basis of their high school ability levels or their grades? Does an able diamond in the educational rough stay in the rough?
5. Which underachievers attain relatively higher educational and occupational status as adults? Which, if any, "recover" and achieve up to the level expected of those possessing their abilities?

Methods of Procedure

SAMPLE

The sample was derived from a panel of 6,720 male and female respondents who were first studied as juniors and seniors in high school in 1965-1966 by Gordon McCloskey, Walter Slocum, and William Rushing at Washington State University and described in detail by Otto, Call, and Spenner (1981). The sample was restudied 13 years later in 1979 by Otto et al. (1981) when the subjects were 28-31 years old.

Original sample. The original sample was drawn from high schools in the state of Washington. Twenty-five high schools in the state were classified into six categories according to their numbers of students, and schools were randomly sampled from each stratum until the proportion of students drawn from that stratum equaled the population total. The sample schools in each stratum were divided into two groups which received two different survey instruments that shared a common core of basic demographic and stratification questions.

Form A emphasized demographic variables; Form B asked for more details about social and psychological factors. Students responding to Forms A and B defined two subsamples which, despite some common variables, were analyzed separately to provide replication and a check on the possibility that certain statistical techniques might capitalize on chance.

Classroom teachers administered the written questionnaires to all juniors and seniors in each school who were present and willing to participate; 86% of the enrolled student body participated. Telephone interviews and written questionnaires were administered to a subsample of students, their high school counselors, and their parents. With occasional exceptions, these data are not included in the present report. School personnel arranged to forward the grades and the scores for IQ, aptitude, or achievement tests from school records for those students who responded to the survey.

Follow-up sample. Otto et al. (1981), working at the Boys' Town Center for the Study of Youth Development, near Omaha, were able to locate 98.2% of the original sample approximately 13 years after high school. Of these, 88.9% provided usable telephone interviews ($N = 5,850$), and mailed questionnaires were completed by 74.7% ($N = 4,916$). The telephone interview concentrated on life history (education, family, military, and employment) and social and psychological measures (attitudes about work, current job, sex role orientation, marriage and family relations). High school transcripts were obtained for all but 10 subjects.

The demographic characteristics of the sample were rather close to those obtained for the state of Washington and for the nation. For example, a distribution of occupations for respondents' fathers was very comparable to males of approximately the same age for both the state of Washington and the nation; survey fathers were slightly more advantaged, perhaps because they were drawn from men with a child in high school as opposed to the state and national data, which are based on all males regardless of family status. The educational attainment for respondents' fathers was also only slightly higher than the national population (e.g., 5% fewer fathers with only some high school and 5% more fathers with some college education). The greatest disparity pertained to race: The survey included only 2% nonwhite persons relative to 4% for the state and 12% for the nation.

No sex-of-subject differences were observed with respect to fathers' occupational status and parental education. However, as is reported frequently (e.g., Hout & Morgan, 1975), females had higher grade averages (2.69 versus 2.40), but attained nearly a year less education by age 30 (13.80 versus 14.58).

The total follow-up sample was 92% urban, 22.7% stopped their education with high school, 40% attended college but did not graduate, 21.2% graduated from college and went no further, and 13.3% did some postgraduate work. Approximately 70% had one marriage since leaving high school and another 15% had two or more marriages. Families averaged between three and four children, Approximately one-fourth experienced active duty in the military. Nearly 97% reported one or more full-time jobs since leaving high school, and nearly 75% worked full-time, 5% worked part-time, and 17% were engaged in other major activities (keeping house, military, school) at the time of follow-up. Extensive details are available in Otto et al. (1981).

QUESTIONNAIRES AND VARIABLES

All of the surveys and questionnaires are printed in their entirety in Otto et al. (1981). We used essentially all of the original survey data, but only small amounts of the follow-up data, and recoded many of the variables from the original questionnaire responses. A list of the names of variables we used can be obtained from the senior author[1] and compared to the original questionnaires in Otto et al. (1981) to determine the recodings and specific definitions.

Some of the outcome variables deserve special mention. Years of education was coded 12 for a high school graduate, 16 for a bachelor's degree, 18 for a master's degree, and 20 for a doctorate. Of course, some people fell between these points, and years of education in vocational and technical schools following high school graduation were not necessarily counted year for year with attendance at colleges and universities. For subjects who attended colleges or universities, we coded the level of educational attainment on an 8-point scale beginning with less than one year of college and ending with a doctorate or other professional degree.

Hourly wage for the first job following high school and for the current job at the time of the follow-up interview consisted of a transformation of wages and salary to an hourly rate. It did not include outside income. Status ratings of the first and current job were determined on the basis of Duncan's (1961) SEI Index. Job satisfaction was measured on a 4-point scale consisting of very or somewhat dissatisfied and fairly or very satisfied.

Selecting Underachievers and Controls

Underachievers were defined according to the regression procedure, and then several comparison groups were created.

DEFINING UNDERACHIEVERS

As indicated above, underachievement is generally defined as school performance, usually measured by grades, that is substantially below what would be predicted on the basis of the student's mental ability, typically measured by intelligence or standardized academic tests.

Mental ability index. Table 4.1 presents the academic and intelligence tests given by the schools in this sample that were used to create the mental ability index we employed. The most frequently used test was the Washington Pre-College Test (WPCT), which was given to 2,981 students in the fall of their senior year. The mean of the verbal and quantitative subtests was used as the mental ability index, hereafter also called simply mental ability.

The WPCT was used as the reference test with scores from other tests transformed to be statistically comparable (same means and variance) to the WPCT if the tests correlated at least .70 with it in this sample and had relatively normal distributions of scores. Those tests, the particular score used, the number of students taking each test, and

TABLE 4.1 Tests used to compose the mental ability index

Test	Score	N	When Given
Washington Pre-College Test	Mean verbal, quantitative	2981	Sr. (100%)
Preliminary Scholastic Aptitude Test	Mean verbal, math	1615	Jr. (81.5%), Sr. (18.5%)
California Test of Mental Maturity	IQ	1288	7th (61.9%), So. (29%)
National Merit Scholarship Qualifying Test	Selection score	1136	Jr. (100%)
Iowa Test of Educational Development	Composite	1047	Jr. (63.3%), Fr. (31.8%)
Scholastic Aptitude Test	Mean verbal, math	769	Jr. (93.2%), Sr. (6.6%)
Otis Quick-Scoring Mental Ability Test	IQ	692	8th (36.5%), So. (26.7%)
National Educational Development Test	Composite	329	So. (69.6%), Fr. (30.4%)
Differential Aptitude Test	Mean verbal, numerical	252	Fr.-So. (44.7%), 8th-Fr. (44.2%)
Kuhlmann-Anderson Intelligence Test	IQ	146	So. (51.8%), Jr. (18.2%)
Lorge-Thorndike Intelligence Test	IQ	97	Jr. (54.5%), Fr. (41.6%)
Henmon-Nelson Test of Mental Ability	IQ	61	Jr. (55.6%), Sr. (31.1%)

the two grades in which the highest percentage of students took the test are given in Table 4.1. Only the School and College Ability Test and the Iowa Test of Basic Skills were not eligible by these criteria. Students often had more than one test score; the score used for the index was determined by a preference sequence that maximized the number of students contributing a test score during their junior or senior years and minimized the number of different tests used.

Ideally, mental ability should be assessed with an IQ test, not academic aptitude or achievement tests, and several IQ tests were included in the set of tests in Table 4.1. Considerable debate focuses on whether a serious difference exists between ability and aptitude tests, and some authorities suggest that the distinction between them is misleading or inconsequential (Humphreys, 1974; Kaplan & Saccuzzo, 1982; Sternberg, 1982). In our data set, the median correlation between IQ or aptitude tests and achievement tests was .75, and the median correlation among achievement tests was .74. Thus, no obvious disparity of individual differences between IQ or aptitude and achievement tests is present in these data.

Grades. High school grade point averages were available, but preliminary analyses indicated that mean grade averages varied between schools. Sex × School mixed model analyses of variance (BMDP3V) showed school effects for both Form A (*chi-square* = 6.80, *df* = 1, $p < .009$) and Form B (*chi-square* = 3.93, *df* = 1, $p = .047$) samples, which differences were still present when the mental ability index was used as a covariate ($ps < .001$). In short, grading practices were different from school to school. Therefore, grade averages were standardized (mean of 0, standard deviation of 1) within each school; these standardized grade averages were used throughout, called simply grades or GPA.

Regression analyses. Regressions of standardized grade point average on the mental ability index were calculated and the results are presented in Table 4.2. The regressions, nearly identical for the two samples, were conducted on males and females combined so that information on the relative sex distribution of underachievement could be obtained.

Definition of Underachiever. The average standard error of estimate for these two regression analyses was .7521. All subjects whose residual standardized grade average was less than –.7521 (i.e., one standard error below the predicted value) were defined to be *Under-*

TABLE 4.2 Regressions of standardized grades on mental ability index

	M	SD	N	r	F	SE
Form A						
Standardized GPA	.00	1.00	1959	.65	1453.11***	.76
Mental Ability	49.15	8.26				
Form B						
Standardized GPA	.00	1.00	2189	.66	1699.43***	.75
Mental Ability	49.17	8.31				

***$p < .05$

achievers. Assuming a normal distribution, this would represent approximately the bottom 16% of students, determined by the discrepancy between their grades and their mental ability.

FORMING COMPARISON GROUPS

An attempt was made to construct three comparison groups to:

1. control for grades while allowing mental ability to be lower but appropriate to those grades (Same GPA)
2. control for mental ability while allowing grade point averages to be consistent with predictions (Same MA)
3. control for mental ability while allowing grades to be much better than predictions (Overachievers)

The strategy (and problems) in selecting these groups are illustrated in Figure 4.1 This represents the hypothetical scatter plot for the regression of standardized grades on the standardized mental ability index. Underachievers (about 15%) are defined to fall one standard error or more below the regression line. So-called Overachievers (about 15%) fall one standard error above the regression line. The non-underachieving comparison pupils are those 15+% who fall closest to the regression line. Some of these have mental ability indices within the range of those of the Underachievers (vertical hatch lines) and compose the Same MA group. Others have grades within the

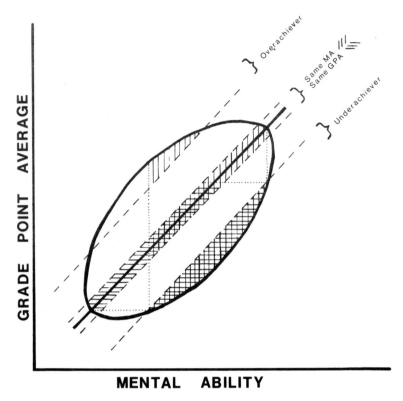

Figure 4.1. Schematic scatter plot of the hypothetical regression of grade point average on mental ability showing the areas from which Underachievers (vertical/horizontal hatching), Same GPA (horizontal), Same MA (vertical), and Overachiever subjects were drawn

range of those of the Underachievers (horizontal hatch lines) and compose the Same GPA group.

Because of a variety of selection biases that occur when Underachievers are picked out of a sample (see below), perfectly matching each Underachiever with a different student in each of the comparison groups was not possible. The following procedures define the comparison groups that came as close as possible to the ideal.

Same grades, appropriate mental ability (Same GPA). Ideally, one wants to locate individuals with the same grades as the Underachievers who are not underachieving. These control subjects would have the same grade averages as the Underachievers, but mental ability scores appropriate for those grades (i.e., the subjects would fall close to the regression line of grades on mental ability). They would control for grades and underachievement, but not for mental ability, which would be lower on the average than for the Underachievers. Such a group is difficult to obtain, because a substantial percentage of students with low grades are underachievers, especially those students who have very poor grade averages (made disastrously low because of their underachievement), and they are disproportionately boys (see below). Therefore, it is to be expected that relatively fewer individuals will be available for the Same GPA than for the Underachiever group, and that a bias toward lower grades will exist among Underachievers relative to the Same GPA group.

The Same GPA comparison subjects were selected in the following way. For each Underachiever, the file was searched for the subject of the same sex, school size, and form (criteria that were never compromised) who was closest in standardized grade point average to the target Underachiever and whose residual standardized grade average (i.e., deviation from the GPA-MA regression line) was small. This search followed these specific instructions:

1. If the Underachiever's standardized grade point average was less than –1.70 (i.e., one standard deviation from the Underachiever mean), select a comparison student with a standardized grade point average as close as possible to the Underachiever's standardized grade point average, but not more than ± .58 from that of the Underachiever (i.e., one standard deviation), *and* who has a residual standardized grade point average between ± .143 (a range that would embrace approximately the central 15% of the distribution of scores about the regression line).

2. If the Underachiever's standardized grade point average is greater than or equal to –1.70, select a student with a standardized grade point average as close as possible to that of the Underachiever, but not more than ± .29 (i.e., one-half the Underachiever's standard deviation), *and* who has a residual standardized grade point average between + .143.

3. If no match is found with the above procedures, process again by the same procedures, but allow the residual standardized grade point average to vary between ± .29 (approximately the central 30% of the distribution around the regression line).

The greater tolerance for deviation from the Underachiever's adjusted grade point average if that average was below –1.70 recognized that variability was greater in the extremes and that a bias existed favoring lower grade averages for Underachievers.

Same mental ability, appropriate grades (Same MA). This comparison group attempted to control for mental ability and underachievement, but not for grades. It embraced students whose mental ability was the same as the Underachievers, but whose grades were more appropriate or closer to what would be expected on the basis of their mental ability. On the average, those grades would be higher than those of the Underachievers. This group presumably represents what the Underachievers would have been like if they had not been underachieving. Because Underachievers had slightly lower mental ability scores than the total population, there was a small tendency for the mental ability scores of the Same MA group to be higher.

The specific procedure was as follows. For each Underachiever, a comparison subject was selected of the same sex, school size, and form (criteria that were never compromised) according to the following instructions:

1. If the Underachiever's mental ability is less than 41 or greater than 57 (i.e., the extreme one-third of the distribution), select a student with a mental ability that is as close as possible to that of the Underachiever, but not more than ± 8 (approximately one standard deviation) from it *and* who has a residual standardized grade average between ± .143 (the central 15%).

2. If the Underachiever's mental ability is either equal to or between 41 and 46 or 52 and 57, select a comparison subject with a mental ability that is as close as possible to that of the Underachiever, but not more than ± 6 of it and whose residual standardized grade average is between ± .143.

3. If the Underachiever's mental ability is between 46 and 52 (the central third of the distribution), select a comparison student with a mental ability that is as close as possible to that of the Underachiever, but not more than ± 4 *and* whose residual standardized grade average is between ± .143.

4. If no match is achieved with the above procedures, repeat them, but allow the residual standardized grade average to be ± .29.

These procedures recognized that a closer match can be obtained in the central regions of a distribution than in the extremes.

Same mental ability, better than expected grades (Overachievers). The final comparison group consisted of individuals who had mental ability scores equivalent to the Underachievers, but grade point averages that substantially exceeded what would be expected on the basis of their mental ability scores. They were *Overachievers.* Subjects were selected within the same sex, school size, and form (criteria that were never compromised) according to the following specific instructions:

1. If the Underachiever's mental ability score was less than 41 or greater than 57, select a student with a mental ability score that is as close as possible to that of the Underachiever, but not more than ± 8 from it *and* whose residual standardized grade point average is greater than .7521 (the upper 15%).
2. If the Underachiever's mental ability is either equal to or between 41 and 46 or 52 and 57, select a student with a mental ability score that is as close as possible to that of the Underachiever, but not more than ± 6 from it *and* whose residual standardized grade average is greater than .7521.
3. If the Underachiever's mental ability is between 46 and 52, select a student with a mental ability that is as close as possible to that of the Underachiever, but not more than ± 4 from it *and* whose residual standardized grade point average is greater than .7521.

It should be noted that the Overachievers were matched approximately for mental ability with the Underachievers, because their primary purpose in this study was to constitute an extremely high performance comparison for the Underachievers—their opposite, in a manner of speaking. The use and interpretation of the Overachievers data will be limited to this purpose. Had Overachievers been a focus of interest in their own right, they would have been selected without this mental ability constraint.

The sequence of selecting comparison subjects. Additional procedures for selecting the comparison subjects included classifying schools as large or small, with large defined to be schools with more than 500 students and small defined to be schools with 500 or fewer students. Schools and subjects within schools were randomly sequenced, and then an attempt was made to match the first Underachiever with a Same GPA comparison subject, then a Same MA comparison subject, and finally an Overachiever. The next Underachiever was first matched with a Same MA comparison subject, then a Same GPA comparison subject, and finally an Overachiever. These two sequences were used alternately throughout the sample. This sequencing was implemented because the Same GPA and the Same MA groups were the most salient controls and because some of the same subjects could be considered potential members of either of these two comparison groups, depending on the particular Underachiever in question. The sequencing procedure would not influence the composition of the Overachiever group, so its sequence in the matching process was not balanced.

Results of the matching. The matching data for these four groups are presented at the left of Table 4.3. The table gives the number of subjects, the mean and standard deviation for mental ability and standardized grade point average, and the test of significance for each group compared to Underachievers separately for males and females within each form.

Note first that over the two forms 444 males, but only 205 females, were identified as Underachievers. Thus, over the entire range of mental ability, somewhat more than two males (2.17) are identified as Underachievers to every female, a ratio that is roughly comparable to a variety of other studies using various definitions of underachievement.

Second, the mean mental ability for Underachievers ranges between 48.14 and 49.94 with a standard deviation between 6.44 and 7.61. These means are roughly comparable to the mean of the entire sample (49.16), but the variability is somewhat less (overall $SD = 8.28$). Although the definition of Underachievers would seem to favor those with higher mental abilities, this is not the case when the regression definition is used. That is, in many studies, underachievers may be underrepresented at the low end of the mental ability distribution

TABLE 4.3 Matching data for achievement groups

								Selected Underachiever Groups						
		Mental Ability			Standardized GPA				Mental Ability			Standardized GPA		
	N	M	SD	F	M	SD	F	N	M	SD	F	M	SD	F
Form A														
Males:														
Underachievers	219	49.66	7.61		−1.14	.61								
Same MA	166	50.71	7.69	1.75	.15	.61	426.78***	166	49.96	8.03	.75	−1.10	.63	339.53***
Overachievers	79	50.32	8.45	.42	1.13	.67	807.81***	79	49.76	7.46	.19	−1.13	.55	535.05***
Same GPA	70	42.67	6.74	44.22***	−.57	.53	46.70***	70	55.39	6.79	123.70***	−.63	.55	.45
Females:														
Underachievers	107	49.94	6.44		−1.08	.52								
Same MA	107	50.20	6.12	.09	.10	.48	284.30***	107	49.94	6.44	.09	−1.08	.52	291.31***
Overachievers	107	49.76	6.35	.05	1.18	.54	1054.26***	107	49.94	6.44	.05	−1.08	.52	972.71***
Same GPA	67	39.60	6.19	111.74***	−.81	.48	11.65***	67	51.79	6.59	121.92***	−.86	.52	.38
Form B														
Males:														
Underachievers	225	48.94	7.27		−1.27	.61								
Same MA	197	50.79	6.73	7.53***	.14	.53	644.36***	197	49.72	7.18	2.35	−1.22	.59	566.56***
Overachievers	80	49.08	7.35	.02	1.06	.62	993.03***	80	48.93	6.87	.02	−1.22	.58	577.55***
Same GPA	80	40.93	5.85	79.01***	−.73	.47	52.44***	80	52.71	5.91	160.66***	−.82	.50	1.25
Females:														
Underachievers	98	48.14	7.22		−1.27	.63								
Same MA	98	48.46	6.93	.10	−.04	.54	238.10***	98	48.14	7.22	.10	−1.27	.63	217.04***
Overachievers	98	48.20	7.26	.00	1.00	.57	816.45***	98	48.14	7.22	.00	−1.27	.63	711.38***
Same GPA	55	39.64	5.02	54.34***	−.81	.43	24.64***	55	51.71	6.31	123.32***	−.88	.50	.65

$***p < .001$

because of statistical and definitional constraints, but when using the regression definition they come from all levels of mental ability and as a group are not different in average mental ability than the population as a whole.

Third, the biases produced by the definition of underachievement were manifested in two ways. The Same MA group tended to have a somewhat higher mental ability than the Underachievers. This occurred for males (significant in Form B), but not females, perhaps because of the substantially greater number of underachieving males. Second, the Same GPA group, in fact, did not have the same grades. In all four sets, the Same GPA group had significantly higher grades than the Underachievers.

Selected Underachievers. These inequities in large part are the expected and inevitable consequences of the nature of underachievement. It is an impossible task to create perfectly matched groups. An alternative is to create an additional set of comparison groups, inevitably biased, but oppositely. Results that concur across both comparisons are unlikely to be the product of the biases.

To correct for our initial imbalance, subsets of the Underachiever group were selected to be matched with individuals in each of the comparison groups. These *Selected Underachiever* groups, whose data are presented at the right of Table 4.3, include only those Underachievers for whom a comparison subject was found when the original comparison groups were formed. The F statistics given in the right portion of the table represent the simple test between the Selected Underachievers and the corresponding comparison group given on the same line at the left.

The data for the Selected Underachievers and the comparison groups are quite satisfactory. In each of the four samples (sex × form), the Selected Underachiever group did not differ significantly in mental ability from its corresponding Same MA and Overachiever groups, but did differ significantly in grades. Conversely, in each of the four samples (sex × form), the Selected Underachievers did not differ significantly in grades from the Same GPA group, but did differ significantly in mental ability. Most Fs for nonsignificant results were less than 1 and all significant Fs were larger than 100. Note in the case of females, because of the smaller number of Underachievers, the Selected Underachiever groups for the Same MA and Overachiever groups were identical to the unselected Underachiever groups (the difference in significance tests derived from the fact that the tests at the left of the table were conducted as specific comparisons within a four-group analysis while the tests at the right were conducted as two-group analyses of variance).

The disadvantage of using only the Selected Underachiever groups for all analyses is that a different Selected Underachiever group is matched with each comparison group. This obviates putting the several Selected Underachiever groups into the same statistical analysis because assumptions of independence are violated by the partial overlap of subjects in these groups. Further, because the Selected Underachiever groups contain different subjects, comparability and generality of comparisons across these groups are threatened. Actually, the issues of noncomparability and generality are probably not problems for some comparisons and a relatively small problem for the remainder. Specifically, for the Same MA group, the Selected Underachiever comparison was only a problem for Form B males, and in that case the Selected Underachievers are only .78 higher in mental ability than the unselected Underachiever group for that sample. For females, the Selected Underachiever group is identical to the unselected Underachiever group.

For the Overachiever comparison, no Selected Underachiever group was statistically necessary, and the Selected and unselected Underachiever groups are exceedingly close in mental ability and grade point average.

The comparison for Same GPA, however, did require adjustment for each of the four samples. Here, generality is an issue. These comparisons will be limited to Underachievers without extremely low grade point averages. One might assume that these omitted Underachievers would have the most unfavorable contemporary characteristics and deleterious outcomes.

Although little emphasis will be placed on the Selected Underachievers groups per se, results will be interpreted only when effects are observed consistently over both Selected and unselected comparisons.

Methodological and Statistical Issues

The methodological and statistical approaches we have taken in this book raise certain issues.

COMPARISON GROUPS

It must be recognized at the outset that although the regression method of defining Underachievers yields distinct advantages over most other approaches, no definition can eliminate the fact that Underachievers come from only certain portions of the grades-on-mental-ability scatter plot, rendering essentially impossible the perfect matching of comparison subjects. Not only will the Same GPA group not control for mental ability and the Same MA group not control for grades, but one-for-one matching of Underachievers with either type of non-underachieving comparison subjects is likely to be impossible.

Our strategy was to use both Same GPA and Same MA comparison groups, the full group of Underachievers, and subsets of Selected Underachievers who indeed were matched one-to-one with comparison subjects. The availability of two partly overlapping forms of the questionnaire permitted replication across two samples for some variables. The interpretive strategy, then, was to emphasize converging trends and deemphasize inconsistencies across the several comparisons. Even so, of course, the results could be messy or uninterpretable, depending upon the consistency in the particular pattern of outcomes. We believe the actual results were relatively homogeneous and interpretable.

ALTERNATIVE APPROACHES

The biases in the matching procedure discussed above illustrate the inherent statistical problems in attempting to control for two variables (MA, GPA) when studying a third variable that is completely determined by them (i.e., the GPA-MA discrepancy called underachievement). These problems stimulate methodologists to suggest other statistical approaches to answering the research questions. We believe that no approach can fully correct the inherent confounding, no approach is without its warts and wrinkles, no approach is obviously better on balance than the one used here, and it is not obvious that the strategy used here biased the results in an obvious way. It should be acknowledged, however, that other valid and reasonable approaches do exist that offer certain apparent advantages.

Regression approaches. One possibility is to use the residual standardized grade average (i.e., the GPA-MA discrepancy) as a metric variable, regress out grades and mental ability, and then see if the residual predicts outcome variables over and above that predicted by grades and mental ability. This method certainly appears simpler and even more direct than the comparison group approach we have taken here. But we were not interested in the entire residual dimension, which includes the full range from Underachievers through Overachievers. Further, who is to say that this is a meaningful psychological dimension? Only the extreme Underachievers are of importance from the standpoint of parents and educational policy.

An alternative would be to assign Underachievers a score of 1 and others 0 and see if this dichotomous variable predicted any residual variance. But comparing Underachievers with *all* others is not a salient comparison. Perhaps one could assign 1 to Underachievers, 2 to Non-Underachievers, and 3 to Overachievers—but now one has essentially the comparison groups as formed here.

Finally, regardless of how the residual is handled, a simple regression strategy fails to deal with the inherent confounding and biases. Variables, for example, would be regressed up and down regression lines that exceed the available data, which would be the consequence of the inherent confounding if the regression approach is used. The regression procedure would hide the inherent warts and wrinkles, not cure them. At least in the comparison groups approach, the imperfections are clear for all to see; conducting a set of comparisons with opposite biases faces the problems squarely and openly, if not perfectly or elegantly.

Structural modeling. Another alternative is structural modeling. Indeed, structural modeling is commonly used by sociologists for analyzing this type of data (e.g., Alexander & Eckland, 1975). Unquestionably, structural equations would provide a more statistically elegant approach, and frequent users of the technique are often ardent in their devotion to the method. Although we do not oppose structural modeling in general and see it as an appropriate strategy for dealing with some kinds of questions, we believe it has certain limitations, especially in the present context.

First, structural modeling requires one and preferably several moderately specific theoretical models that can be compared (Appelbaum & McCall, 1983). In our judgment, such models or the theory on which to base them do not exist for underachievement. Even in the sociological field of status attainment for unselected samples, investigators who use structural modeling to analyze data similar to those available here admit that educational attainment, a major outcome variable for our study, is "influenced by a sizable number of antecedent factors, none of which is clearly predominant" (Alexander & Eckland, 1975, p. 187), implying the lack of a clear model. Further, no guarantee exists that models formulated during the study of status attainment for unselected samples will apply to underachievers, youths who, by definition, are exceptions (i.e., statistical "error") to the ability-grades relationship that is often a crucial component of such models.

Second, partial correlational techniques would not solve the lack of comparability we faced in creating the comparison groups any more than do the regression procedures considered above (from which they are derived). Although it appears that results are obtained after "controlling" for other variables that are correlated with the main predictors, it is still possible—even likely, we would argue—that different subjects contribute disproportionately more to some relationships than to others and that functionally different subjects are controlling for different variables—witness our difficulty finding one-to-one matches for all underachiever comparison groups.

Third, structural modeling produces results that are more statistically abstract and more difficult to interpret and understand, especially from a practical standpoint, than those obtained by using comparison groups. We would never argue that simple but deceptive methods are better than complicated but accurate ones, but it was not clear, given the above argument, that the complicated methods were more accurate in this case.

Fourth, our questions were relatively simple. We wanted to know if underachievers attained educational and occupational status commensurate with their grades or with their abilities and which variables predicted who would or would not attain up to ability level. We were less interested, at least at this point, in which variables had direct versus indirect influence on this result, for example.

Finally, we believe our decision not to use structural modeling was not contradicted by the results actually obtained. In retrospect, we perceive no major finding derived from our conventional group comparisons that is likely to be questioned because we did not use structural modeling. The results were relatively uniform, consistent, and straightforward, even though ample opportunity existed for the complicated, messy, and uninterpretable findings that might be clarified by structural modeling.

We do not claim to have solved in any perfectly satisfying way the major methodological problems discussed here. We would argue, however, that we have tried to deal with the issues of comparison groups and statistical analyses more intensively than have most others represented in the literature to date, and that a study potentially is more useful if such an attempt is made than if these issues are ignored or no comparisons are conducted at all, as has typically been the case in the study of underachievement.

Note

1. Robert B. McCall, Director, Office of Child Development, 2017 Cathedral of Learning, University of Pittsburgh, Pittsburgh, PA 15260.

Are Underachievers
Different in High School?

In this chapter we examine whether Underachievers are different than comparison groups on a large number of variables measured during high school.

Metric Variables

The first set of analyses was aimed at determining the ordinal ("metric") variables assessed during high school that discriminated between Underachievers and the other groups.

ANALYSES

A total of 30 items from the high school questionnaire for Form A and 28 from Form B produced scales with at least ordinal properties. These variables were individually analyzed with a four-group analysis of variance comparing Underachievers, Same MA, Overachievers, and Same GPA. This was followed by pair-wise comparisons between the Underachievers and each of the other three groups, and finally pair-wise comparisons between Selected Underachievers and each of the three comparison groups. Multivariate analyses, which might have brought more order to the results, were precluded because the data missing within subjects reduced the sample size drastically if four or more variables were included in a single analysis.

Admittedly, all these comparisons are complicated, but they are necessary to deal with the inherent imbalance between groups. To simplify drawing conclusions, interpretive emphases will be placed on those variables that display significant differences for both selected and unselected comparisons, across forms (if they were asked on both forms), and across sex, although systematic differences between the sexes were interpreted as sex differences, not failures to replicate.

The results are presented in Tables 5.1 to 5.4. These tables give the variable in the left column. Then the means are presented for Underachievers, Same MA, Overachievers, and Same GPA groups, with the significance level for the pair-wise comparison with Underachievers following the mean and the significance level for the pair-wise comparison with Selected Underachievers preceding the mean. Numbers in parentheses represent the number of cases in each group for that particular variable.

The tables present only those variables for which a significant four-group comparison was obtained for the indicated sex and form. Variables marked with a dagger were significant for both sexes; those listed for one sex, but not the other were significant for that sex, but not the other sex. Some tested variables were not found to be significant for either sex. For Form A, these included status of father's occupation, mid-parent education, family attitude toward education, abilities for desired occupation, probability of realizing desired occupation, status of expected occupation, differences between status ratings for occupational aspirations and expectations, and work preparation. For Form B, variables showing no significant difference for either sex included importance of getting ahead, relationship with father, relationship with mother, relationship with parents, and locus of control.

MAIN THEMES

The significant results presented in Tables 5.1 to 5.4 reveal two general themes.

TABLE 5.1 Significant differences between groups for contemporary variables, males, Form A

Variable	Underach.	Same MA	Overach.	Same GPA
		Mean (Ns)		
Interest in schoolwork†	3.53	***3.89***	***4.04***	3.54
	(218)	(166)	(79)	(70)
Activity offices held†	.78	***1.52***	***2.02***	1.16
	(177)	(136)	(67)	(61)
Percent academic subjects†	.75	***.79***	***.81***	+.75
	(194)	(154)	(77)	(65)
Satisfaction with school†	17.18	***18.30***	***19.22***	+17.22
	(213)	(162)	(79)	(69)
Academic activities†	6.50	*7.07**	***7.49***	6.25
	(207)	(163)	(79)	(65)
Nonacademic activities†	9.43	***10.44***	+10.49*	+10.43*
	(207)	(163)	(79)	(65)
Activities†	20.58	***22.44***	***22.52***	21.51
	(207)	(163)	(79)	(65)
School ability†	27.79	***31.12***	***33.45***	*28.25
	(214)	(162)	(77)	(68)
General competence†	18.06	**19.04**	***19.79***	17.98
	(204)	(152)	(76)	(63)
Friends' valuation of education†	34.70	***38.34***	***39.24***	37.00+
	(188)	(147)	(71)	(62)
Thought about educational plans†	3.28	*3.42*	***3.49*	3.31
	(210)	(161)	(77)	(70)
Educational aspirations†	3.20	***3.98***	***4.43***	3.83***
	(216)	(163)	(79)	(70)
Educational expectation†	3.08	***3.80***	***4.10***	3.56**
	(217)	(163)	(79)	(69)
Status of desired occupation†	59.11	**68.23***	**69.78***	60.28
	(184)	(146)	(72)	(57)
Difference between educational aspirations and expectation†	0.19	0.28	0.39+	*0.46*
	(215)	(162)	(79)	(69)

†Significant for both sexes.
Numbers in parentheses indicate the Ns for that group.
Asterisks following a mean is significance level for pair-wise comparison with Underachievers.
Asterisks preceding a mean is significance level for pair-wise comparison with Selected Underachievers.
+, *, **, *** = $p < .10, .05, .01, .001$, respectively.

TABLE 5.2 Significant differences between groups for contemporary variables, females, Form A

	Mean (Ns)			
Variable	Underach.	Same MA	Overach.	Same GPA
Family Income	3.31	3.29	**3.60**	3.36
	(105)	(103)	(105)	(66)
Interest in schoolwork†	3.60	***3.99***	***4.28***	3.70
	(107)	(107)	(107)	(66)
Activity offices held†	1.10	+1.532+	***2.08***	1.07
	(82)	(921)	(96)	(55)
Number of friends	5.54	*4.67*	5.27	5.30
	(93)	(93)	(92)	(47)
Percent academic subjects†	.69	**.72**	***.73***	.71
	(92)	(103)	(105)	(60)
Satisfaction with school†	17.60	***18.98***	***19.90***	17.34
	(106)	(100)	(104)	(64)
Academic activities†	6.60	***7.59***	***8.52***	6.62
	(102)	(106)	(107)	(66)
Nonacademic activities†	9.97	*10.84*	***11.64***	10.85*
	(102)	(106)	(107)	(66)
Activities†	21.72	***23.91***	***25.93***	22.62
	(102)	(106)	(107)	(66)
School ability†	28.25	***31.07***	***34.42***	*27.17
	(106)	(105)	(103)	(65)
General competence†	16.91	***18.94***	***19.74***	16.63
	(96)	(99)	(104)	(57)
Self-esteem	33.96	*35.53*	***37.46***	34.16
	(102)	(98)	(105)	(61)
Friends' valuation of education†	36.34	***39.70***	***42.50***	36.91
	(91)	(96)	(98)	
Thought about educational plans†	3.51	3.55	**3.72**	3.37
	(104)	(106)	(107)	
Educational aspirations†	2.89	***3.57***	***3.99***	2.92
	(102)	(105)	(107)	(67)
Educational expectation†	2.76	***3.42***	***3.89***	2.81
	(106)	(103)	(107)	(67)
Abilities for expected occupation	3.80	3.90	***4.13***	3.85
	(93)	(96)	(99)	
Parents' attitude toward desired occupation	4.19	4.30	*4.42*	*4.47*
	(97)	(100)	(102)	(58)

(Continued)

TABLE 5.2 (Continued)

Variable	Underach.	Same MA	Overach.	Same GPA
		Mean (Ns)		
Parents' attitude toward	4.24	4.27	*4.48*	*4.51*
expected occupation	(84)	(90)	(89)	(57)
Status of desired	51.00	***61.33***	***60.74***	52.91
occupation†	(97)	(96)	(98)	(55)
Status of expected	50.84	55.91	***62.80***	50.11
occupation	(51)	(55)	(65)	(28)

†Significant for both sexes.
Numbers in parentheses indicate the Ns for that group.
Asterisks following a mean is significance level for pair-wise comparison with Underachievers.
Asterisks preceding a mean is significance level for pair-wise comparison with Selected Underachievers.
$^{+}$, *, **, *** = $p < .10, .05, .01, .001$, respectively.

Differences between groups almost solely reflected differences in grades rather than differences in mental ability. Almost all the significant differences were between Underachievers and Same MA and between Underachievers and Overachievers, groups that differed on high school grades but were matched on mental ability. Rarely was a significant difference found between both unselected and Selected Underachievers and the Same GPA group, which had the same grades but lower mental ability than the Underachievers, and none of those that did were significant for both sexes.

There was relative consistency in which variables showed significant differences across the sexes within a form. Thirteen of 15 variables that revealed group differences for males and 13 of 21 such variables for females in Form A were also significant for the other sex. The variables that were significant for females and not for males tended to involve social relations (e.g., number of friends), parental approval for future plans (parents' attitude toward desired or expected occupation), self-esteem, and desire for and expectation of a high-status job. For Form B, 17 of 20 significant variables for males were also significant for females and 17 of 20 significant variables for females were also significant for males. Again, variables significant for females but not for males tended to involve social factors (i.e., bothered by low

TABLE 5.3 Significant differences between groups for contemporary variables, males, Form B

Variable	Underach.	Same MA	Overach.	Same GPA
		Mean (Ns)		
Number of schools attended†	2.44 (225)	+2.22+ (197)	*2.16+ (80)	**2.04* (79)
Socioeconomic status of family†	4.00 (220)	*4.18* (193)	4.15 (78)	4.05 (76)
Family's status in community	6.17 (222)	***6.69*** (189)	+6.61* (77)	6.25 (75)
Status of father's occupation†	40.35 (179)	***51.86*** (171)	44.47 (62)	41.73 (67)
Midparent education†	3.09 (220)	***3.57*** (193)	**3.58*** (79)	3.13 (79)
School activities†	1.53 (188)	**2.18*** (182)	**2.81*** (74)	1.80 (74)
Dating habits†	3.51 (221)	+3.23* (194)	*2.92** (77)	3.45 (75)
IPAT anxiety	30.99 (122)	**25.81** (67)	+25.00* (28)	28.23 (31)
School ability compared to peers†	3.30 (218)	***3.78*** (183)	***4.04*** (77)	+3.34 (77)
Quality of schoolwork†	3.17 (213)	***3.69*** (183)	***3.78*** (77)	*3.24 (76)
Grade capability†	3.99 (215)	***4.34*** (184)	***4.60*** (76)	4.00 (75)
Estimate father's grade of actual work†	3.16 (216)	***3.75*** (183)	***3.96*** (73)	3.32+ (71)
Desired family status†	7.19 (218)	***8.10*** (193)	**7.92*** (76)	7.61+ (75)
Educational aspirations†	3.09 (222)	***4.10*** (195)	***4.36*** (80)	3.32 (79)
Educational expectation†	2.86 (216)	***3.87*** (191)	***4.13*** (78)	3.20* (78)
Ability to complete college†	3.75 (223)	***4.34*** (196)	***4.48*** (80)	3.95+ (80)
Perceived father's estimate of ability for college†	3.92 (210)	***4.36*** (187)	***4.58*** (74)	4.14+ (74)
Occupational aspirations†	56.62 (167)	***69.74*** (168)	***69.72*** (68)	58.88 (67)
Occupational expectation†	55.76 (117)	***68.01*** (126)	**72.71*** (49)	55.29 (45)

(Continued)

TABLE 5.3 (Continued)

Variable	Underach.	Same MA	Overach.	Same GPA
		Mean (Ns)		
Difference between status ratings for occupational aspirations and expectations	3.14	0.55	[+]−4.56	1.54

†Significant for both sexes.
Numbers in parentheses indicate the Ns for that group.
Asterisks following a mean is significance level for pair-wise comparison with Underachievers.
Asterisks preceding a mean is significance level for pair-wise comparison with Selected Underachievers.
[+], [*], [**], [***] = $p < .10, .05, .01, .001$, respectively.

opinions of abilities, siblings happier than subject, and perceived father's estimate of grade capability).

Relative to students having the same mental ability, but lower grades that closely matched their abilities (i.e., Same MA), Underachievers had lower opinions of their abilities, took fewer academic subjects, participated in fewer activities, held fewer offices in extracurricular activities, and had lower educational and occupational desires and expectations. These themes were present for both males and females in both forms. Underachievers in Form B, but not in Form A came from families with less education and less social status. Underachievers of both sexes in Form B (the relevant question was not asked in Form A) showed more involved dating and heterosexual relationships than the Same MA group or Overachievers. These results tend to show that Underachievers are not systematically different than other students with the same grades.

Categorical Variables

The categorical variables were analyzed with a series of simple chi-square tests using the same general testing strategy employed

TABLE 5.4 Significant differences between groups for contemporary variables, females, Form B

		Mean (Ns)		
Variable	Underach.	Same MA	Overach.	Same GPA
Number of schools attended†	2.35	2.40	*1.95*	2.56
	(98)	(97)	(97)	(55)
Socioeconomic status of family†	3.99	4.10	**4.26*	3.98
	(96)	(93)	(98)	(55)
Status of father's occupation†	34.31	***46.35***	*42.00*	39.98
	(84)	(82)	(86)	(43)
Midparent education†	2.86	**3.33**	**3.31**	2.90
	(96)	(96)	(96)	(53)
School activities†	1.80	***2.87***	***3.56***	+2.60**
	(89)	(92)	(88)	(50)
Dating habits†	4.30	**3.58**	***3.33***	3.82+
	(95)	(95)	(91)	(54)
Bothered by low opinions of abilities	1.92	*2.19*	*2.15*	2.14+
	(93)	(91)	(93)	(50)
Siblings happier than subject	3.89	**4.62**	**4.67***	+4.32
	(88)	(81)	(84)	(44)
School ability compared to peers†	3.14	***3.45***	***3.89***	*3.08
	(92)	(92)	(93)	(50)
Quality of schoolwork†	3.17	***3.57***	***3.70***	3.22
	(90)	(89)	(90)	(50)
Grade capability†	3.86	***4.18***	***4.58***	+3.83
	(89)	(90)	(93)	(48)
Perceived father's estimate of grade capability†	4.11	*4.34*	***4.59***	**3.98
	(89)	(94)	(95)	(52)
Perceived father's grade of actual work†	3.22	***3.82***	***3.99***	3.39
	(93)	(91)	(95)	(51)
Desired family status†	7.05	*7.54*	**7.66**	7.22
	(94)	(95)	(96)	(55)
Educational aspirations†	2.60	***3.57***	***3.66***	2.84
	(96)	(98)	(97)	(55)
Educational expectation†	2.34	***3.35***	***3.55***	2.60
	(97)	(98)	(95)	(55)
Ability to complete college†	3.42	***4.19***	***4.27***	3.47
	(98)	(98)	(97)	(55)
Perceived father's estimate of ability for college†	3.87	**4.29***	***4.47***	4.10
	(93)	(94)	(97)	(52)

(Continued)

TABLE 5.4 (Continued)

		Mean (Ns)		
Variable	Underach.	Same MA	Overach.	Same GPA
Occupational aspirations†	44.80	***62.16***	***59.42***	†52.79*
	(80)	(80)	(77)	(42)
Occupational expectations†	48.03	***59.09***	***58.31***	48.05
	(74)	(82)	(74)	(37)

†Significant for both sexes.
Numbers in parentheses indicate the Ns for that group.
Asterisks following a mean is significance level for pair-wise comparison with Underachievers.
Asterisks preceding a mean is significance level for pair-wise comparison with Selected Underachievers.
$^{+}$, *, **, *** = $p < .10, .05, .01, .001$, respectively.

above for the metric variables. The general trend of the results was also the same.

MAIN THEMES

Generally, the contemporary characteristics of Underachievers were more closely associated with their grades than with their mental ability. As for the metric variables, when the four-group analysis was significant, the pair-wise comparisons between Underachievers and Same MA and between Underachievers and Overachievers were significant. In contrast, only a few individual comparisons between Underachievers and Same GPA were significant. This tendency was true across sex and form.

Form A. The significant results for males and females for Form A are presented in tables 5.5 and 5.6, respectively. These tables give the significance level associated with the four-group test followed by the significance level for the pair-wise tests between Underachievers and Same MA, Underachievers and Overachievers, and Underachievers and Same GPA. The final column contains a brief description of the nature of the difference. A dash means that the test was not significant, and a probability value in parentheses represents the probability of

TABLE 5.5 Contemporary discriminators of Underachievers for categorical variables, males, Form A: Significance level of comparison

Variable	Four-Group	Same MA	Overach.	Same GPA	Nature of Difference
Size of community	.012	.066	.001	—	Underach. more likely from big cities
Thought about work preparation†	.053	.020	—	—	Underach. less likely to prepare
Counselor's judgment of subject's achievement (N_{Total} = 105)†	.000	.002	.000	—	Underach. judged to be underachieving more than other groups
Liked physical education courses	.041	.062	.070	— (.042)	Underach. liked PE courses more
Liked vocational courses	.000	.000	.005	—	Underach. liked vocational courses more frequently
Liked math/science courses†	.000	.000	.000	—	Underach. liked math/science courses less frequently

†Significant for both sexes.
Numbers in parentheses are for a comparison with Selected Underachievers when it differed from the unselected Underachievers comparison.

the test between the group indicated at the top of the column and the Selected Underachievers. The latter information is included only when the significance of the difference for Selected Underachievers was not the same as the test involving the unselected Underachievers.

Relative to students in the Same MA and Overachiever groups, Underachievers of both sexes had thought less about their future careers and preferred less academic courses (physical education and vocational courses for boys and applied courses for girls), especially avoiding math and science. Underachieving males were more likely to come from big cities, but this was not replicated in Form B. Underachieving females were more likely than any comparison group to say that the probability of realizing their desire as to occupation was improbable to nil. Relative to Same MA, Underachieving females had

TABLE 5.6 Contemporary discriminators of Underachievers for categorical
variables, females, Form A: Significance level of comparison

Variable	Four-Group	Same MA	Overach.	Same GPA	Nature of Difference
Thought about work preparation†	.020	.038	.004	—	Underach. less likely to prepare
Probability of realizing desired occupation	.001	.034	.108	.002	Underach. more likely to say it was totally improbable
Mother's employment outside home	.039	.019	—	—	Underach. mothers worked less
Person expecting greatest achievement	.013	—	.034	.057	Overach. fathers expected most
Counselor's judgment of subject's achievement ($N_{Total} = 80$)†	.005	.020	.001	—	Underach. judged to be underachieving more than other groups
Liked applied courses	.001	.002	.004	—	Underach. liked applied courses more frequently
Liked math/science courses†	.000	—	.000	—	Underach. liked math/science courses less frequently

†Significant for both sexes.

mothers who were *less* likely to be working, a result counter to current suspicions.

No significant differences for either sex were observed for 15 variables: race, abilities for desired occupation, willing to train for desired occupation, father's and mother's attitudes toward desired occupation, parents' marital status, number of siblings, birth order, size and nature of father's employer, father's and mother's education, friends seen individually or in a group, whether close friends dropped out of high school, liked no school courses, and liked arts and humanity courses.

Form B. The significant results for Form B are presented in tables 5.7 and 5.8.

Relative to Same MA and Overachievers, Underachievers of both sexes were less likely to be in the academic track of the curriculum, they estimated that their father judged their grade capability to be lower, and they were more likely to suggest that their mother understood their problems an average amount than either extreme. Male Underachievers were more likely to have extremely close or extremely distant relationships with their fathers and, to a lesser extent, with their mothers.

Relative to all groups, female Underachievers were more likely to be the youngest and less likely to be the oldest child in their families, and fewer had mothers who always were easy to talk with and always understood their problems.

Twelve variables showed no differences for either sex: number of siblings, race, parents' marital status, size and nature of the father's employer, employed in past year, importance of getting ahead, parent of greatest personality resemblance, father is easy to talk with, mother or father is warm and affectionate, mother's expression of love, and talking to mother helps.

COUNSELORS' JUDGMENTS

The school counselors' judgment of whether a student was an overachiever, average, or an underachiever was of special interest, although this information was available for only a relatively small number of cases in Form A (see Otto et al., 1981). For both males and females, counselors detected correctly only one-half the Underachievers, but they were even worse at correctly identifying Overachievers (33.3% of the males and 10.5% of the females). They were best at judging students who performed appropriately for their mental ability, although this is to be expected because this was the largest group. Thus, even though they may have had access to test scores, the counselors were not particularly skilled at identifying Underachievers and even worse at picking Overachievers. Alternatively, they may

TABLE 5.7 Contemporary discriminators of Underachievers for categorical variables, males, Form B: Significance level of comparison

Variable	Four-Group	Same MA	Overach.	Same GPA	Nature of Difference
Curriculum track†	.000	.000	.000	—	Underach. less likely to be in academic track than general, vocational, commercial
Size of community	.006	.053	.041 (.113)	—	Underach. more likely live in country than Same MA and more likely from 10-50K than Overach.
Father understands problems	.047	.074	.020 (.104)	—	Underach. fathers were less likely to understand problems
Perceived father's estimate of grade capability†	.000	.000	.000	—	Underach. perceived fathers to have lower grade estimate
Father's expression of love	.022	.054 (.061)	.013	—	Underach. fathers expressed love less frequently
Closeness to father	.005	.062 (.018)	.077	—	Underach. had extremely close or distant relationship to father
Talking to father helps	.007	.007	—	—	Underach. had extremes in talking with father
Mother understands problems†	.032	.049 (.061)	—	—	Underach. had extremes in mother understanding
Closeness to mother	.000	.005	—	.025	Underach. had extremes in closeness versus Same MA but less close versus Same GPA

†Significant for both sexes.
Numbers in parentheses are for a comparison with Selected Underachievers when it differed from the unselected Underachievers comparison.

TABLE 5.8 Contemporary discriminators of Underachievers for categorical variables, females, Form B: Significance level of comparison

Variable	Four-Group	Same MA	Overach.	Same GPA	Nature of Difference
Curriculum track†	.000	.000	.000	—	Underach. less likely in academic track
Birth order	.006	.001	.021	.023	Underach. more likely youngest and less likely oldest child
Perceived father's estimate of grade capability†	.000	.003	.000	.038	Underach. lower (esp. Cs & Ds), but more As than Same GPA
Mother understands problems†	.024	—	.004	.071 (.032)	Underach. fewer "always" responses
Mother easy to talk with	.026	—	—	.047	Underach. fewer "always" and "sometimes" responses

†Significant for both sexes.
Numbers in parentheses are a comparison with Selected Underachievers when it differed from the unselected Underachievers comparison.

not have paid attention to or had confidence in mental test scores. This result suggests that if it is important to detect underachievers, some systematic method other than counselors' judgments should be used.

Dimensions and Syndromes

Generally, underachievers differ from students with the same mental ability, but not from students with the same grades, and these results were substantially replicated across form and sex. Two additional analyses were conducted for the purpose of refining the interpretation of these differences.

FACTOR ANALYSIS

Although multivariate analyses were precluded because of missing data, missing data factor analyses of the significant metric group discriminators were conducted separately for each form and sex group to help integrate the significant discriminators and facilitate interpretation. In each of the four analyses, the first principal component consisted of relatively high loadings for each of the variables (e.g., .30 to .85). The Varimax rotated factors were more discriminating, and were generally quite similar across form and sex.

The main themes among the metric variables that distinguished between Underachievers and the Same MA group across form and sex included lower future educational and occupational aspirations and expectations and lower perception of current and future educational abilities, general competence, and self-esteem for the Underachievers.

Girls tended to have more factors than boys. One additional theme was a social dimension (e.g., number of friends, friends' valuation of education, and number of activities) in Form A or a mixing of such variables, their parent's perceptions of abilities, and other factors (Form B). The other additional theme for girls was the separation of educational from occupational aspirations and expectations. These differences seem to reflect the proposition that social relations and parental opinions are more intimately tied to achievement for girls than boys, and that education and occupational achievement were less related for girls than boys (at least in the years when these assessments were conducted). The results from the two forms differed in that two additional factors were present for both sexes in Form B: parent educational and occupational status and a mixture of parents' and the student's own desired future status. These variables tended not to discriminate between groups for Form A subjects.

Generally, the categorical variables that discriminated between Underachievers and Same MA subjects were consistent with these themes. In Form B, a number of variables pertaining to relationships with parents were significant, but a composite variable composed of all the items pertaining to parental relationships was analyzed as a metric variable and did not discriminate between the groups for either sex. Thus, although some aspects of the Underachiever's relationship to parents may be involved, a general difference was not found.

TYPES OR SYNDROMES OF UNDERACHIEVEMENT

A major goal of our research was to determine more objectively than has been done in the past whether underachievers as a group consisted of a few major types or syndromes, as some have theorized in the clinical literature (see chapters 1 and 2).

To describe such types, variables were selected from the high school surveys that reflected major characteristics of underachievers based upon the literature, theory, and our data. Exploratory factor analyses (using missing data correlations) suggested major dimensions that characterized Underachievers, and variables were selected that represented those dimensions and had minimum missing data (clustering requires complete data). For Form A, the variables included educational aspirations, interest in school work, mental ability, activities, work attitude, family attitude toward education, mid-parent education, and self-esteem. For Form B, the variables were educational aspirations, dating habits, importance of getting ahead, perceived father's estimate of grade capability, mental ability, midparent education, and internality (locus of control).

The subjects were clustered on the basis of these variables separately for form and sex by two different clustering routines (Overall & Klett, 1972, p. 207; SAS computer package). Neither analysis produced satisfactory results; that is, they did not generate a small set of clusters embracing most of the subjects. For example, the SAS procedure placed only one-third of the total available subjects (203 of 649) into 10 or 11 male and 7 or 8 female clusters per form containing medians of five males and three females each. Moreover, the means of each cluster did not describe obvious or intuitive types.

These results did not accomplish the purpose of defining a few major types that contained most Underachievers. Two major explanations are possible. First, Underachievers are a very heterogeneous group, especially when the entire range of abilities is included, and they are not accurately characterized by a few types or syndromes.

Second, the variables did not capture the main dimensions along which types actually vary. Of course, fewer variables will necessarily yield fewer and larger clusters, but given our data set and procedures, Underachievers did not fall into a few large types or syndromes.

Conclusions

These analyses converge on the following conclusions.

First, generally, underachievers are different from non-underachieving students with the same mental ability on a variety of variables, but they were very similar to non-underachieving students with the same grades but lower mental ability. Grades have already reflected the underachiever's motivational problems, so the question arises as to whether underachievement is any different than simply poor grades, an issue to be addressed in the remaining chapters.

Second, relative to students of the same mental ability, underachievers had lower opinions of their abilities, took fewer academic subjects (especially math and science), participated in fewer activities and held fewer offices in them, had lower educational and occupational desires and expectations and had thought less about their future careers, had lower opinions of their competence, had more involved heterosexual relationships, and perceived their fathers to have a lower opinion of their academic capability.

Third, the differences between underachievers and students with the same mental ability were very similar for males and females. The one exception focused on peer and parental relations: Female underachievers had fewer friends and less parental support for their desired occupations, they were more likely to be the youngest child in their families, and they had somewhat distant relationships with their mothers.

Fourth, school counselors were relatively insensitive to identifying underachievers and performed dismally at identifying overachievers (especially females), so any systematic attempt to detect underachievers should rely on more than counselor judgments.

Fifth, an attempt to define different qualitative syndromes of underachievement was not successful, either because none exist or because the variables relevant to such syndromes were not available.

Sixth, some variables that did not discriminate between groups were notable because they are often mentioned as factors in underachievement (see literature review in chapter 2). Underachievers, in comparison to the Same MA group, were not different in terms of race, marital status of parent, number of siblings, birth order, and parental education, although the latter two variables did differentiate groups in Form B. Thus, when underachievement is defined across the entire range of abilities, it is not confined to upper- or middle-class, white, or later-born youths rebelling against their very achieving parents and siblings, although such parents may be more likely to be concerned and bring the problem to the attention of school personnel. Underachievers from less-educated families and racial minorities may not be perceived as underachievers by parents, counselors, or the students themselves; the perception may be not of low grades, but of unusually high test performance.

6

Are Underachievers Different 13 Years After High School?

Subjects in the four groups (Underachievers, Same MA, Overachievers, Same GPA) were compared with respect to the status rating of first job, hourly wage or income from first job, years of formal education, status rating of current job, hourly wage or income from current job, and satisfaction with current job. "First job" was the first full- or part-time employment following high school, and "current job" was that most recently held at the time of the follow-up interview approximately 13 years after high school.

Major Outcome Measures

Because the educational and occupational outcome measures were available for both Forms A and B, these data were analyzed with a groups × forms multivariate analysis variance performed separately for males and females with either the two first-job or the four current-job dependent variables. Where no interactions between groups and forms are noted, the reader may assume that the effects discussed were parallel for both forms (i.e., replicated across forms). Following the four-group multivariate analysis, a priori multivariate pair-wise analyses compared Underachievers with Same MA, Underachievers with Overachievers, and Underachievers with Same GPA. Then these pair-wise analyses were repeated using the Selected Underachievers. Once again, although this was complicated, interpretative emphasis is placed on effects that are significant across the Selected-unselected comparisons and across forms where possible.

FIRST JOB

The results were essentially identical for males and females and showed that the status and income of the students' first jobs paralleled their grades, not their mental abilities. Underachievers had lower status and lower paying jobs than the Same MA and the Overachievers groups, but no differences were reported between Underachievers and Same GPA. These results held whether the pair-wise comparisons were made on the unselected or on the Selected Underachiever groups, and no result was qualified by an interaction with form. The complete results are presented in tables 6.1 and 6.2.

As a group, then, Underachievers did not attain a first job commensurate in status or income with their mental ability, but found employment consistent with their underachieving school performance.

LONG-TERM EDUCATIONAL AND OCCUPATIONAL OUTCOME

The results for analyses on attained education and occupation 13 years after high school were similar to those for the first job and comparable for males and females and for the two forms. In general, Underachievers completed years of education and held jobs with incomes and status that matched their high school grades rather than their mental abilities. That is, they were poorer than Same MA, but similar to Same GPA students. There were no group differences for the dependent variable of job satisfaction, either because individuals in the four groups were equally satisfied with their jobs or because the measure itself was not very discriminating (only four categories of response were available).

Males. For males, the multivariate statistical comparisons were quite consistent in showing that the four groups differed with respect

TABLE 6.1 Status and income of first job as a function of group, males, Forms A and B

					Underachievers Selected to Match the		
	Under-achiever (N = 394)	Same MA (N = 315)	Over-achiever (N = 144)	Same GPA (N = 132)	Same MA (N = 322)	Over-achiever (N = 139)	Same GPA (N = 135)
Status	27.34	39.97	47.85	28.81	27.99	25.55	29.41
Income	4.11	4.90	5.45	4.41	4.18	4.05	4.50

Comparisons		F_{mult}	df	p
Four Groups				
	Multivariate	17.11	6,1952	.000
	Status	34.63	3,977	.000
	Income	6.57	3,977	.000
Underachiever vs. Same MA				
Unselected	Multivariate	25.37	2,704	.000
	Status	49.92	1,705	.000
	Income	10.04	1,705	.002
Selected	Multivariate	19.83	2,632	.000
	Status	39.33	1,633	.000
	Income	7.16	1,633	.008
Underachiever vs. Overachiever				
Unselected	Multivariate	44.30	2,533	.000
	Status	86.86	1,534	.000
	Income	17.11	1,534	.000
Selected	Multivariate	31.04	2,278	.000
	Status	61.94	1,279	.000
	Income	9.25	1,279	.003
Underachiever vs. Same GPA				
Unselected	Multivariate	0.71	2,521	.490
	Status	0.52	1,522	.471
	Income	1.22	1,522	.269
Selected	Multivariate	0.04	2,262	.960
	Status	0.05	1,263	.816
	Income	0.05	1,263	.820

TABLE 6.2 Status and income of first job as a function of group, females, Forms A and B

	Under-achiever (N = 163)	Same MA (N = 174)	Over-achiever (N = 162)	Same GPA (N = 104)	Underachievers Selected to Match the		
					Same MA (N = 163)	Over-achiever (N = 163)	Same GPA (N = 99)
Status	39.26	45.75	53.23	37.89	39.26	39.26	42.69
Income	2.43	2.84	3.36	2.64	2.43	2.43	2.50

Comparisons		F_{mult}	df	p
Four Groups				
	Multivariate	12.50	6,1188	.000
	Status	20.60	3,595	.000
	Income	11.62	3,595	.000
Underachiever vs. Same MA				
Unselected	Multivariate	7.29	2,332	.001
	Status	9.83	1,333	.002
	Income	8.26	1,333	.004
Selected	Multivariate	7.29	2,332	.001
	Status	9.83	1,333	.002
	Income	8.26	1,333	.004
Underachiever vs. Overachiever				
Unselected	Multivariate	32.06	2,320	.000
	Status	46.71	1,321	.000
	Income	35.59	1,321	.000
Selected	Multivariate	32.06	2,320	.000
	Status	46.71	1,321	.000
	Income	35.59	1,321	.000
Underachiever vs. Same GPA				
Unselected	Multivariate	1.31	2,262	.273
	Status	0.34	1,263	.561
	Income	1.93	1,263	.166
Selected	Multivariate	2.39	2,198	.094
	Status	3.58	1,199	.060
	Income	0.61	1,199	.435

to the set of variables of years of formal education and income, status, and satisfaction with their job at follow-up. Univariate tests were significant for all dependent variables except job satisfaction. These results occurred for the four-group analysis and for the pair-wise analyses comparing Underachievers with the Same MA and Over-achievers, and they were consistent whether the unselected or the Selected Underachievers were used in the comparison. In contrast, no consistent effects were observed between Underachievers and the Same GPA group. The statistical details are presented in Table 6.3. Form by group interactions are reported in the footnotes to the table, but in no case did they alter the conclusions stated above.

As can be seen from the table, Underachieving males completed 1.63 years of formal education (10.5%) less and earned 76 cents less per hour (7.7%) than the Same MA students. The social status of their current job was substantially less as well.

Females. The results for females were similar except the effect on income was not as consistent. In general, Underachieving females completed 1.05 years of education (7.4%) less, earned 73 cents less per hour (12.2%), and held substantially lower status jobs than the Same MA females. Although the percentage of income difference was greater for females than for males, the statistical significance was less for females because of the wide variability caused by women whose careers were interrupted by childbearing and other circumstances. Again, job satisfaction was not related to group affiliation, and no differences on any outcome variable were observed between Under-achievers and Same GPA. Further, all effects reported were similar regardless of whether the unselected or Selected Underachievers were used in the comparison. The details are presented in Table 6.4.

BAD START OR SLOW PROGRESS?

Were the long-term educational and occupational outcomes simply extensions of the differences found for the first job, or was educational and occupational progress since the first job also related to group membership?

TABLE 6.3 Long-term educational and occupational follow-up as a function of group, males, Forms A and B

					Underachievers Selected to Match the		
	Under-achiever (N = 390)	*Same MA* (N = 319)	*Over-achiever* (N = 145)	*Same GPA* (N = 131)	*Same MA* (N = 323)	*Over-achiever* (N = 141)	*Same GPA* (N = 133)
Years of Education	13.96	15.59	16.27	14.34	13.97	13.64	14.21
Income	9.06	9.82	10.85	9.65	8.86	8.51	8.93
Status	41.65	54.40	60.99	45.45	42.19	40.52	47.10
Satisfaction	2.20	2.17	2.15	2.27	2.19	2.13	2.09

Comparisons					F_{mult}	*df*	*p*
Four Groups*							
	Multivariate				17.38	12,2577	.000
	Years of Education				67.98	3,977	.000
	Income				5.12	3,977	.002
	Status				31.13	3,977	.000
	Satisfaction				0.94	3,977	.422
Underachiever vs. Same MA							
Unselected**	Multivariate				31.02	4,702	.000
	Years of Education				117.81	1,705	.000
	Income				4.64	1,705	.032
	Status				50.34	1,705	.000
	Satisfaction				0.51	1,705	.476
Selected	Multivariate				28.19	4,635	.000
	Years of Education				105.68	1,638	.000
	Income				6.92	1,638	.009
	Status				41.76	1,638	.000
	Satisfaction				0.18	1,638	.669
Underachiever vs. Overachiever							
Unselected	Multivariate				41.99	4,528	.000
	Years of Education				147.30	1,531	.000
	Income				15.29	1,531	.000
	Status				74.19	1,531	.000
	Satisfaction				0.82	1,531	.367
Selected	Multivariate				36.02	4,279	.000
	Years of Education				132.98	1,282	.000
	Income				15.54	1,282	.000
	Status				56.91	1,282	.000
	Satisfaction				0.05	1,282	.823

(Continued)

TABLE 6.3 (Continued)

					Underachievers Selected to Match the		
	Under-achiever (N = 390)	Same MA (N = 319)	Over-achiever (N = 145)	Same GPA (N = 131)	Same MA (N = 323)	Over-achiever (N = 141)	Same GPA (N = 133)
Years of Education	13.96	15.59	16.27	14.34	13.97	13.64	14.21
Income	9.06	9.82	10.85	9.65	8.86	8.51	8.93
Status	41.65	54.40	60.99	45.45	42.19	40.52	47.10
Satisfaction	2.20	2.17	2.15	2.27	2.19	2.13	2.09

Comparisons					F_{mult}	df	p
Underachiever vs. Same GPA							
Unselected***	Multivariate				1.64	4,514	.163
	Years of Education				3.90	1,517	.049
	Income				1.81	1,517	.179
	Status				2.56	1,517	.110
	Satisfaction				0.89	1,517	.346
Selected	Multivariate				1.67	4,257	.157
	Years of Education				0.30	1,260	.586
	Income				1.69	1,260	.195
	Status				0.30	1,260	.586
	Satisfaction				3.99	1,260	.047

*Four-group: Form × Group: Form A more years education except Same MA, $F = 2.51$, $df = 12,2577$, $p = .003$; years of education only significant, $F = 4.10$, $df = 3,977$, $p = .007$.
**Same MA: Form × Group: Form A more years of education except Same MA, $F = 2.71$, $df = 4,702$, $p = .029$; years of education only significant $F = 9.33$, $df = 1,705$, $p = .002$.
***Same GPA, Form × Group: Form A higher for Underachievers on status and satisfaction; Form B higher for Same GPA on status and satisfaction; $F = 3.45$, $df = 4,514$, $p = .009$; Status = $F = 4.94$, $df = 1,517$, $p < .027$; Satisfaction = $F = 4.86$, $df = 1,517$, $p < .028$ (only case in which Underachievers vs. another group was not same for two forms).

Multivariate analyses of covariance were performed on all pairwise comparisons of unselected and Selected Underachievers versus Same MA, Overachievers, and Same GPA using the social status and income of the first job as covariates and years of formal education, income, job status, and satisfaction with the current job as dependent variables. Presumably, if group differences emerged in these covariance analyses, they would indicate that following the first job, Underachievers progressed in education and the job market at slower rates than the comparison groups.

TABLE 6.4 Long-term educational and occupational follow-up as a function of group, females, Forms A and B

					Underachievers Selected to Match the		
	Under-achiever (N = 151)	Same MA (N = 159)	Over-achiever (N = 167)	Same GPA (N = 91)	Same MA (N = 151)	Over-achiever (N = 151)	Same GPA (N = 89)
Years of Education	13.18	14.23	15.14	13.38	13.18	13.18	13.39
Income	5.27	6.00	6.22	5.21	5.27	5.27	5.47
Status	44.83	53.94	57.83	45.91	44.83	44.83	46.06
Satisfaction	2.11	2.16	2.25	2.18	2.11	2.11	2.07

Comparisons					F_{mult}	df	p
Four Groups							
	Multivariate				9.81	12,1474	.000
	Years of Education				35.62	3,560	.000
	Income				2.70	3,560	.045
	Status				16.32	3,560	.000
	Satisfaction				0.90	3,560	.440
Underachiever vs. Same MA							
Unselected	Multivariate				9.62	4,303	.000
	Years of Education				27.70	1,306	.000
	Income				2.49	1,306	.116
	Status				19.52	1,306	.000
	Satisfaction				0.24	1,306	.624
Selected	Multivariate				9.62	4,303	.000
	Years of Education				27.70	1,306	.000
	Income				2.49	1,306	.116
	Status				19.52	1,306	.000
	Satisfaction				0.24	1,306	.624
Underachiever vs. Overachiever							
Unselected	Multivariate				27.26	4,311	.000
	Years of Education				97.03	1,314	.000
	Income				9.38	1,314	.002
	Status				37.42	1,314	.000
	Satisfaction				2.56	1,314	.111
Selected	Multivariate				27.26	4,311	.000
	Years of Education				97.03	1,314	.000
	Income				9.38	1,314	.002
	Status				37.42	1,314	.000
	Satisfaction				2.56	1,314	.111

(Continued)

TABLE 6.4 (Continued)

					Underachievers Selected to Match the		
	Under-achiever ($N = 151$)	Same MA ($N = 159$)	Over-achiever ($N = 167$)	Same GPA ($N = 91$)	Same MA ($N = 151$)	Over-achiever ($N = 151$)	Same GPA ($N = 89$)
Years of Education	13.18	14.23	15.14	13.38	13.18	13.18	13.39
Income	5.27	6.00	6.22	5.21	5.27	5.27	5.47
Status	44.83	53.94	57.83	45.91	44.83	44.83	46.06
Satisfaction	2.11	2.16	2.25	2.18	2.11	2.11	2.07
Comparisons					F_{mult}	df	p
Underachiever vs. Same GPA							
Unselected	Multivariate				0.38	4,235	.821
	Years of Education				0.90	1,238	.343
	Income				0.03	1,238	.865
	Status				0.16	1,238	.694
	Satisfaction				0.38	1,238	.541
Selected	Multivariate				0.36	4,173	.840
	Years of Education				0.00	1,176	.973
	Income				0.35	1,176	.557
	Status				0.00	1,176	.962
	Satisfaction				0.90	1,176	.345

Males. For males, the covariance results presented in Table 6.5 were quite consistent with the results for the unadjusted long-term educational and occupational outcomes reported above. That is, Underachievers were less accomplished in years of education, income, and job status at follow-up even after adjusting for the characteristics of their first job compared to the Same MA and Overachiever groups. No effects were observed for job satisfaction. Notice that while the univariate *F* for income was not significant for the unselected Underachievers compared to the Same MA group, it was significant for the Selected Underachievers in this comparison.

Generally, for males, no significant differences were observed between Underachievers and the Same GPA group. However, this comparison was subject to an interaction with form, especially with respect to the job status measure. As can be seen in Table 6.5, a

TABLE 6.5 Long-term educational and occupational follow-up after covarying the status and income of first job, males, Forms A and B

Comparisons		F_{mult}	df	p
Underachievers vs. Same MA				
Unselected	Multivariate	16.62	4,640	.000
	Years of Education	63.97	1,643	.000
	Income	2.57	1,643	.109
	Status	17.03	1,643	.000
	Satisfaction	0.03	1,643	.857
Selected	Multivariate	15.99	4,577	.000
	Years of Education	58.67	1,580	.000
	Income	4.72	1,580	.030
	Status	13.71	1,580	.000
	Satisfaction	0.18	1,580	.670
Underachievers vs. Overachievers				
Unselected	Multivariate	18.76	4,489	.000
	Years of Education	69.06	1,492	.000
	Income	5.53	1,492	.019
	Status	20.22	1,492	.000
	Satisfaction	0.01	1,492	.920
Selected	Multivariate	16.02	4,256	.000
	Years of Education	59.63	1,259	.000
	Income	5.26	1,259	.022
	Status	15.04	1,259	.000
	Satisfaction	0.69	1,259	.408
Underachievers vs. Same GPA				
Unselected*	Multivariate	1.19	4,476	.315
	Years of Education	2.42	1,479	.121
	Income	1.19	1,479	.277
	Status	1.47	1,479	.226
	Satisfaction	1.39	1,479	.239
Selected	Multivariate	1.96	4,239	.101
	Years of Education	0.19	1,242	.666
	Income	2.39	1,242	.124
	Status	0.56	1,242	.454
	Satisfaction***	4.63	1,242	.033
Form A	Multivariate	1.20	4,232	.312
	Years of Education	1.66	1,235	.199
	Income	0.03	1,235	.873
	Status	0.70	1,235	.405
	Satisfaction	0.80	1,235	.371

(Continued)

TABLE 6.5 (Continued)

Comparisons		F_{mult}	df	p
Form A Selected	Multivariate	1.17	4,113	.329
	Years of Education	0.19	1,116	.666
	Income	0.34	1,116	.559
	Status	3.55	1,116	.062
	Satisfaction	0.00	1,116	.993
Form B**	Multivariate	2.98	4,239	.020
	Years of Education	0.75	1,242	.387
	Income	1.56	1,242	.213
	Status	6.15	1,242	.014
	Satisfaction	6.21	1,242	.013
Form B Selected	Multivariate	2.72	4,121	.033
	Years of Education	1.34	1,124	.249
	Income	2.44	1,124	.121
	Status	0.62	1,124	.434
	Satisfaction	8.98	1,124	.003

*Group x Form: F_{mult} = 2.96, df = 4,476, p < .020; Years of Education and Income, Fs < 1; Status, F = 5.21, df = 1,479, p = .023; Satisfaction, F = 5.51, df = 1,479, p = .019.
**Underachievers vs. Same GPA Form B means:
　　Status—39.02 vs. 47.26
　　Satisfaction—2.13 vs. 2.38
***Underachievers lower for Form B only.

significant multivariate difference between Underachievers and Same GPA was observed for Form B, but not for Form A; Underachievers in Form B held substantially lower status jobs than the Same GPA group. This general multivariate effect was also present where the Selected Underachievers were used for this comparison, although the univariate significance of individual dependent variables depended upon whether unselected or Selected Underachievers were compared. Therefore, these data provide a hint that some male Underachievers may show less progress after their first job in terms of job satisfaction and possibly in job status than those students who had the same high school grades, but lower mental abilities (Same GPA).

Females. The covariance analyses for females (Table 6.6) showed Underachievers doing less well than either Same MA or Overachievers with respect to years of education and job status, but not income

TABLE 6.6 Long-term educational and occupational follow-up after covarying the status and income of first job, females, Forms A and B

Comparisons		F_{mult}	df	p
Underachievers vs. Same MA				
Unselected	Multivariate	5.32	4,267	.000
	Years of Education	14.77	1,270	.000
	Income	0.49	1,270	.484
	Status	9.84	1,270	.002
	Satisfaction	0.27	1,270	.601
Selected	Multivariate	5.32	4,267	.000
	Years of Education	14.77	1,270	.000
	Income	0.49	1,270	.484
	Status	9.84	1,270	.002
	Satisfaction	0.27	1,270	.601
Underachievers vs. Overachievers				
Unselected	Multivariate	16.73	4,267	.000
	Years of Education	60.59	1,270	.000
	Income	2.34	1,270	.127
	Status	17.05	1,270	.000
	Satisfaction	2.49	1,270	.116
Selected	Multivariate	16.73	4,267	.000
	Years of Education	60.59	1,270	.000
	Income	2.34	1,270	.127
	Status	17.05	1,270	.000
	Satisfaction	2.49	1,270	.116
Underachievers vs. Same GPA				
Unselected	Multivariate	0.72	4,208	.579
	Years of Education	0.57	1,211	.450
	Income	0.64	1,211	.424
	Status	0.24	1,211	.624
	Satisfaction	1.01	1,211	.317
Selected	Multivariate	0.50	4,157	.730
	Years of Education	0.02	1,160	.900
	Income	0.70	1,160	.400
	Status	0.17	1,160	.680
	Satisfaction	0.92	1,160	.340

and job satisfaction. No effects for income or job satisfaction were observed, and no differences between Underachievers and Same GPA were observed. All significant results occurred whether unselected or Selected Underachievers were involved. Again, Underachievers progressed more slowly following their first job with respect to years of education and job status relative to students who had the same mental ability but whose grades were appropriate (Same MA).

Specific Outcomes

The analyses of major outcome variables described above were followed by more detailed investigations of type of postsecondary schools attended, likelihood of completing 4 years of college, number of different jobs held, and divorce rate.

TYPES OF POSTSECONDARY EDUCATION

The above analyses indicate that Underachievers completed fewer years of education after high school than did the Same MA and Overachievers groups. This effect was investigated in greater detail by testing the percentage of students in each of the four groups who ever attended various types of schools as well as the success of those who did attend a college or university. The dependent variables were (1) the percentages of each group who ever attended vocational or technical school, professional school, junior or community college, business school, secretarial school, nursing school, or a college or university; (2) the percentages of those students who ever attended a college or university who dropped out, graduated and stopped their education, or graduated and attended postgraduate school; (3) the percentage ever serving in the military; (4) the percentage ever married; (5) the average number of jobs held since high school; (6) the percentages who took a part-time first job or held a part-time job upon follow-up; and (7) the percentages who were very or somewhat satisfied or fairly or very dissatisfied with their most recent job at follow-up.

Chi-square analyses were performed on a sample combining Forms A and B and then on Forms A and B separately as well as on unselected and then Selected Underachievers. A four-group analysis was followed by individual comparisons between Underachievers and the other three groups. The significance levels of the obtained chi-squares are presented in Table 6.7 for males and Table 6.8 for females for those dependent variables producing some significant results. Variables described above which do not appear in these tables did not have significant results that were uniform across forms.

The most consistent significant results occurred for the percentage of each group ever attending different types of schools (with the exception of business, secretarial, and nursing schools, for which the percentages were too small to produce significant differences). In addition, progress in a college or university was significantly different for the four groups; however, in pair-wise comparisons, Underachievers differed from the Same MA and the Overachieving groups, but not from the Same GPA group.

Males. The percentages of each group attending different schools are given in Table 6.9 for both males and females for the combined samples of Forms A and B. Although Underachievers and Same GPA were roughly comparable, Underachievers were substantially different from the Same MAs and the Overachievers. Relative to the Same MA group, male Underachievers were almost twice as likely to go to a vocational or technical school, more than one-third as likely to attend a professional school, about as likely to attend a junior or community college, but only half as likely to attend a college or university. Further, of those who did attend a college or university, twice as many Underachievers dropped out and only half as many graduated. Underachievers were 50% more likely to enter the military.

Females. The results were similar for females, but the magnitude of the differences was not quite as great, partly because of the generally higher or lower percentages of females in various categories. Relative to the Same MA group, Underachievers were 57% more likely to go to vocational or technical school, about as likely to go to junior or

TABLE 6.7 Long-term educational and occupational results for categorical variables, males

Variable	Form		4-Grp	Same MA	Over-achiever	Same GPA	Nature of Differences
Vocational/	A&B	Unsel	.001	.004	.001	.056	Underachievers
technical school		Sel	—	.002	.000	.093	twice as likely
attendance							to attend voca-
	A	Unsel	.264	.230	.119	.200	tional/technical
		Sel	—	.273	.148	.346	as Same MA.
	B	Unsel	.002	.004	.003	.136	
		Sel	—	.002	.000	.159	
Professional	A&B	Unsel	.000	.002	.000	.576	Underachievers
school		Sel	—	.005	.000	.743	less likely to
attendance							have gone to
	A	Unsel	.000	.061	.000	.512	professional
		Sel	—	.199	.000	1.000	school.
	B	Unsel	.046	.016	.030	.891	
		Sel	—	.006	.053	.567	
Junior or	A&B	Unsel	.000	.122	.000	.901	Underachievers
community		Sel	—	.282	.001	.117	more likely to
college							attend junior or
attendance	A	Unsel	.010	.023	.002	.078	community
		Sel	—	.053	.007	.608	college.
	B	Unsel	.001	.958	.001	.134	
		Sel	—	.761	.025	.009	
College or	A&B	Unsel	.000	.000	.000	.017	Underachievers
university		Sel	—	.000	.000	.383	less than half as
attendance							likely to attend
	A	Unsel	.000	.000	.000	.003	college or
		Sel	—	.000	.000	.861	university.
	B	Unsel	.000	.000	.000	.565	
		Sel	—	.000	.000	.177	

(Continued)

TABLE 6.7 (Continued)

Variable	Form		4-Grp	Same MA	Over-achiever	Same GPA	Nature of Differences
College outcome	A&B	Unsel	.000	.000	.000	.092	Underachievers twice as likely to drop out, half as likely to graduate as Same MA.
		Sel	—	.000	.000	.869	
	A	Unsel	.000	.000	.000	.026	
		Sel	—	.000	.000	.833	
	B	Unsel	.000	.000	.000	.780	
		Sel	—	.000	.000	.522	
Military service	A&B	Unsel	.000	.000	.000	.498	Underachievers more likely to serve in military.
		Sel	—	.000	.000	.863	
	A	Unsel	.000	.001	.000	.973	
		Sel	—	.021	.000.	233	
	B	Unsel	.000	.000	.000	.343	
		Sel	—	.000	.000	.381	
Number of jobs	A&B	Unsel	.004	.063	.003	.053	Underachievers more likely to change jobs frequently.
		Sel	—	.175	.032	.589	
	A	Unsel	.089	.021	.382	.083	
		Sel	—	.083	.316	.277	
	B	Unsel	.012	.548	.006	.294	
		Sel	—	.582	.139	.303	

community college, and only 42% as likely to attend a college or university. Of those who did attend a college or university, Underachievers were 42% more likely to drop out before graduation.

Conclusion. In summary, Underachievers were dramatically less likely to attend a college or university and, if they did attend, they were much more likely to drop out before graduation than students of comparable mental ability who earned high school grades

TABLE 6.8 Long-term educational and occupational results for categorical variables, females

Variable		Form	4-Grp	Same MA	Over-achiever	Same GPA	Nature of Differences
Vocational/	A&B	Unsel	.001	.051	.001	.610	Underachievers
technical school		Sel	—	.051	.001	.434	more likely to
attendance							attend voca-
	A	Unsel	.625	.694	.507	.531	tional/technical
		Sel	—	.694	.507	.310	school.
	B	Unsel	.000	.002	.000	.818	
		Sel	—	.002	.000	.874	
Professional	A&B	Unsel	.009	.319	.008	.194	Underachievers
school		Sel	—	.319	.008	.318	less likely to
attendance							attend profes-
	A	Unsel	.287	—	.157	.204	sional school.
		Sel	—	—	.157	.316	
	B	Unsel	.024	.321	.025	—	
		Sel	—	.321	.025	—	
Junior or	A&B	Unsel	.041	.430	.785	.014	Underachievers
community		Sel	—	.430	.785	.003	more likely to
college							attend junior or
attendance	A	Unsel	.001	.069	.635	.000	community
		Sel	—	.069	.635	.000	college than
							Same GPA.
	B	Unsel	.811	.447	.366	.540	
		Sel	—	.447	.366	.502	
College or	A&B	Unsel	.000	.000	.000	.182	Underachievers
university		Sel	—	.000	.000	.461	half as likely to
attendance							attend college/
	A	Unsel	.000	.000	.000	.707	university.
		Sel	—	.000	.000	.371	
	B	Unsel	.000	.000	.000	.102	
		Sel	—	.000	.000	.956	

(Continued)

TABLE 6.8 (Continued)

Variable		Form	4-Grp	Same MA	Over-achiever	Same GPA	Nature of Differences
College outcome	A&B	Unsel	.000	.000	.000	.089	Underachievers
		Sel	—	.000	.000	.579	more likely to
							drop out, one-
	A	Unsel	.000	.000	.000	.006	third as likely to
		Sel	—	.000	.000	.043	graduate as Same
							MA.
	B	Unsel	.000	.060	.000	.655	
		Sel	—	.060	.000	.355	
Number of jobs	A&B	Unsel	.006	.205	.000	.072	Underachievers
		Sel	—	.205	.000	.015	more likely to
							change jobs
	A	Unsel	.010	.531	.001	.050	frequently.
		Sel	—	.531	.001	.032	
	B	Unsel	.529	.323	.105	.612	
		Sel	—	.323	.105	.433	

appropriate to that ability. Underachievers were not different in this regard from students with the same high school grades but lower mental ability.

COMPLETING COLLEGE

The educational future of Underachievers also can be expressed by the likelihood of completing 4 years of college. The percentages of such students in each group combined across Forms A and B are given in Table 6.10 for males and females. The four-group and most of the pair-wise chi-squares were significant. Note that the ratios between groups are roughly similar for males and females, although the absolute values are lower for females, which decreased significance levels.

For the sexes combined, the Underachiever had only one chance in five of completing 4 years of college whereas the student of comparable mental ability, but with appropriate grades had better than one

TABLE 6.9 Percentages of each group attending different schools, Forms A and B

Ever Attended	Under-achievers	Same MA	Over-achievers	Same GPA
Males				
Vocational/technical school	14.1	7.5	4.4	8.1
Professional school	2.5	7.0	12.6	3.4
Junior or community college	59.6	54.2	39.0	59.1
College or university	37.9	74.3	88.1	49.0
Drop out	67.2	32.5	22.7	56.5
Graduate and stop	19.4	38.0	40.3	27.4
Graduate plus postgraduate	13.4	29.5	37.0	16.1
Military	54.9	35.5	27.0	51.7
Females				
Vocational/technical school	19.3	12.3	8.3	21.7
Professional school	0.0	0.5	3.4	0.8
Junior or community college	42.1	38.2	43.4	28.3
College or university	23.3	54.9	71.2	30.0
Drop out	83.6	58.9	38.1	69.8
Graduate and stop	10.2	30.4	34.7	19.0
Graduate plus postgraduate	6.2	10.8	27.3	11.1

chance in two of completing college—a likelihood two-and-half times greater. Moreover, in contrast to most other comparisons with the Same GPA group (which were not significant), Underachievers were somewhat less likely to complete college than young people with the same grades, but lower mental ability. The latter group had approximately a one-third greater likelihood of completing 4 years of college than the Underachievers.

This result is important because it is relatively consistent, it pertains to a crucial outcome variable that is widely believed to have important life consequences, and it reveals Underachievers to be at a disadvantage even with respect to students obtaining the same grades with lower mental ability. This finding presumably reflects the continuing influence of the psychological factors involved in underachievement and represents the first sign that underachievement is a syndrome apart from simple grade average.

TABLE 6.10 Estimated likelihood of completing 4 years of college, Forms A and B

	Underachievers	*Same MA*	*Overachievers*	*Same GPA*
Males	24.9%	***62.6%***	***74.8%***	36.2%**
Females	10.4%	32.0%***	***53.2%***	***15.8%
Sexes combined	20.4%	***51.5%***	***62.6%***	**27.1%*

All four-group chi-squares, $p < .001$.
Asterisks following a percentage is significance level for pair-wise comparison with Underachievers.
Asterisks preceding a percentage is significance level for pair-wise comparison with Selected Underachievers.
*, **, *** = $p < .05, .01, .001$, respectively.

NUMBER OF JOBS

There was a tendency for Underachievers to hold more different jobs in the 13 years after high school than all the other groups, but as can be seen from tables 6.7 and 6.8 above, the significance levels of the differences were not uniform across the various comparisons. Thus, although both four-group analyses of Forms A and B combined showed a highly significant difference, that difference was inconsistently expressed across forms and groups and depended on whether unselected or Selected Underachievers were used in the comparison. Therefore, there is some, but inconsistent, evidence that Underachievers display less job stability than either Same MA or Same GPA groups. This is a second sign that Underachievers were distinct from students with comparable grades.

DIVORCE

The consequences of underachievement for personal and social life are displayed in terms of the likelihood of divorce. These percentages for Forms A and B combined for the four groups are given in Table 6.11 separately for males, females, and combined sexes. The results are most emphatic for females; essentially the same relative result occurred for males but with lower absolute rates.

TABLE 6.11 Divorce rates by sex and achievement group, Forms A and B

	Underachievers	Same MA	Overachievers	Same GPA
Males	25.4%	+18.2%*	20.7%	17.5%+
Females	51.4%	***28.0%***	***18.9%***	**34.2%**
Sexes combined	34.0%	***22.1%***	***19.6%***	*22.2%**

Four-group chi-squares are $p < .10$ for males, $p < .001$ for females, $p < .001$ for combined sex-sample.
Asterisks following a percentage is significance level for pair-wise comparison with Under-achievers.
Asterisks preceding a percentage is significance level for pair-wise comparisons with Selected Underachievers.
+, *, **, *** = $p < .10, .05, .01, .001$, respectively.
Cases of separation, death, and cohabitation are included in the total cases.

Combining sexes, Underachievers were 50% more likely to divorce in the 13 years following high school than the other groups, and the divorce rate for Underachieving females was an especially high 51%—twice that of the Underachieving males. Again, contrary to previous results, Underachievers were more likely to divorce than students with the same grades but lower mental ability (Same GPA), a result further supporting the idea of a distinct syndrome of under-achievement.

Conclusion

Generally, underachievers attain the same adult educational and occupational status as non-underachieving youths with the same grades, but lower mental ability. As a group across all mental ability levels, underachievers do not catch up to what would be expected on the basis of their ability. Moreover, underachievers are worse than Same MA and Same GPA comparison youths in three respects: (a) they are less likely to complete 4 years of college, (b) some are likely to change jobs more frequently, and (c) they are much more likely to divorce. It appears, then, that underachievement is a syndrome that is different from poor grades, and that its characteristics persist well into adulthood.

7

Which Underachievers Catch Up to Their Abilities?

The intent for this set of analyses was to identify which high school variables predicted relative educational and occupational success for Underachievers and, in particular, to determine if at least some Underachievers caught up to their ability levels in terms of educational and occupational accomplishments.

Predictors of Relative Success

This book is part of a series on individual differences, and it contributes to this theme in two ways. First, although treated as a group to this point, Underachievers represent an individual difference—they are the lower extremes of the grades-ability disparity. Now we explore the second type of individual difference—variations in educational and occupational outcome within the Underachievement group.

Our first analyses were directed at identifying variables that predicted relative educational and occupational success within the Underachiever group. We then used these results to determine if some

Underachievers attained adult status equivalent to what would be predicted on the basis of their abilities.

GENERAL STATISTICAL APPROACH

The first step was to correlate all variables assessed during high school that had at least ordinal properties with the educational and occupational outcome variables separately for each of the seven groups (the four focal groups plus the three Selected Underachievers). Three main trends emerged. First, significant correlations were almost totally restricted to the outcome variables of years of education, current job status, and current job income. Few relations were found for job satisfaction, perhaps because of the limited 4-point scale used to measure it. Second, if a significant correlation was observed within one group, there was a marked tendency for the correlation to be significant within the other groups. Isolated significant correlations occurred that were not shared by the other groups, but these did not follow a particular pattern. In short, predictions to educational and occupational outcomes generally were not unique to Underachievers or any other group. Third, as a set, correlations for the Underachievers were as high as or slightly higher than for any other group.

The second step of the general approach was to select those high school variables that showed consistent relations to outcome measures across the groups, within either of the two forms, and for either males or females. As a result, two sets of high school variables, one for Form A and one for Form B, were identified for subsequent analysis.

The third step was to enter these selected variables into stepwise multiple regression analyses with each of the three major outcome variables (years of formal education, current job status, and current income). The statistical significance of such regression analyses was not of interest, because the variables were selected on the basis of their correlations with the criteria. What was of interest was the relative importance of different predictors and the amount of variability in the outcome measure associated with them. This and subsequent steps were carried out only on the Underachievers, because they were the group of primary conceptual and practical interest.

The first stepwise analysis entered adjusted grade point average as the first variable, primarily to serve as a covariate. The previous analyses had shown grade point average to be the primary predictor, and regressing GPA placed the conceptual focus of these analyses on the predictive role of high school variables over and above the student's actual grade point average. Therefore, the partial correlations between each of the selected variables and the outcome measures were determined with grade point average adjusted for different high schools and controlled. In general, as expected, these partial correlations were lower than the simple correlations, but only occasionally was the partial *r* not significant when the simple correlation was significant.

EFFICIENT PREDICTORS

The details of the results of these analyses can be obtained from the senior author,[1] but Table 7.1 shows a summary of the major variables that made significant stepwise predictions of educational and occupational outcomes for Underachievers as a function of form and sex after adjustment was made for grade point average.

For Underachieving males, those with higher educational expectations and parents with relatively more education ultimately completed more years of education than other Underachievers, even after years of education was adjusted for high school grade point average. A similar theme occurred less consistently for females, and it was mixed with either the number of activities (Form A) or the youth's perceived ability to complete college (Form B). The social status of the Underachiever's job 13 years after high school was related primarily to educational expectation (Form A males) or occupational aspirations (Form B males, Form A females). Except for Form A males, the income of this job was not predicted by these variables.

Interpretation. It appears that even after adjustments are made for grade point average, underachieving high school students who expected to go to college and to graduate, who had parents who were relatively more educated and perhaps valued education more highly, who believed they were sufficiently competent to complete college,

TABLE 7.1 Variables that predict educational and occupational outcomes for Underachievers (after covarying adjusted GPA; based on stepwise multiple regression)

	Form A Males	Form B Males
Years of education	Educational expectation Midparent education	Educational expectation (Midparent education)
Job status	Educational expectation	Occupational aspirations Activities
Job income	Occupational aspirations Interest in school work General competence	—

	Form A Females	Form B Females
Years of education	Midparent education Activities (Educational expectation)	Educational expectation Ability to complete college
Job status	Occupational aspirations	—
Job income	—	—

Variables in parentheses were the next variable to be entered. Although they contributed nonsignificant additional variance to the prediction of the criterion, they are included here if the same variable did contribute significantly for another group.

who displayed relatively more interest in academic schoolwork, who participated in school and nonschool activities (and presumably achieved some social and achievement successes in those contexts), and who had some degree of self-esteem and self-confidence were likely to achieve relatively more years of postsecondary education. This collection of characteristics is most efficiently indexed by the student's educational expectation and parents' education level. Note these are the same high school variables that distinguished Underachievers from the Same MA group, except that grades now have been partialed out.

From another perspective, one might suppose that students who underachieve because of lack of current commitment to school, because they are emphasizing other activities (e.g., sports), and because they are preoccupied with having a good time, but who nevertheless value education highly, expect to pursue it in the future, and are not crippled by lack of self-confidence or self-esteem are likely to do better educationally in the years following high school. Conversely, high school underachievers who do not value education, dislike school and academic pursuits, are uninvolved in activities, and lack self-confidence are far less likely to succeed at postsecondary education. These characteristics are efficiently represented in the youth's educational expectation and the parents' education level for males and by those variables plus measures of perceived competence and participation in activities for females. Once again, females seem to have a social factor related to achievement that is less pronounced for males.

The interpretation for job status seems similar to that for years of education. Underachieving students with high educational expectations and occupational aspirations who participate in activities and perceive themselves as generally competent are later more likely to obtain higher status jobs than other Underachievers. This predictive pattern is somewhat clearer for males than for females, and the predictions as to years of education were twice as strong as to job status.

THE SPECIAL ROLE OF SELF-ESTEEM, LOCUS
OF CONTROL, AND SUCCESS EXPERIENCES

The clinical literature on Underachievers stresses that such youths have low self-esteem, few success experiences to give them self-confidence and feelings of self-worth, and a tendency toward externality (e.g., luck) with respect to locus of control. This set of variables might be viewed as "perceived competence." Direct or indirect measures of these variables were available and were part of the analyses described above. The analyses were stepwise in nature, and the results did not single out these variables from the total set as most predictive of the outcome measures. This fact does not mean that they are not functional, so we went on to conduct analyses exploring their role directly.

Statistical approach. The Form A questionnaire included a 10-item self-esteem scale and the Form B questionnaire a 10-item locus of control scale (with high scores reflecting internal locus of control). We took participation in activities, available in both questionnaires, as an indirect measure partly reflecting success experiences and social disposition. In Form A, this included activities in and out of school, but in Form B, only activities in school.

In a manner similar to that described above, we repeated stepwise regression analyses to predict relative educational or occupational success for Underachievers, but deliberately entered the self-esteem and activity index (Form A) or the locus of control (hereafter called internality) and activity index (Form B) simultaneously in the second step after adjusted grade point average. The remaining variables in the selected sets were then entered individually in stepwise fashion. In each case, the next variables entered by the analysis turned out to be the same variables that the previous analysis selected as the major predictors when self-esteem, locus of control, or activities were not forced into the equation in a prior step.

Results. For Form A, activities and self-esteem were significantly related to years of education for both males and females, but they did not account for nearly as much variance as the primary predicting variables (i.e., educational expectation and midparent education) even when the primary predicting variables were entered second (i.e., after covarying activities and self-esteem). For example, activities and self-esteem accounted for 5.6% of the variance for males, versus 15% for the two primary predictors, which were entered in the next step. The corresponding figures for females were 10.2% versus 20.4%, indicating that it is possible that self-esteem and activities (or social functions) are somewhat more important for females than for males in predicting years of education. The amount of variance associated with activities and self-esteem in predicting job status or income for both sexes was quite modest and nonsignificant in most cases.

The results for Form B were less consistent. For males, we observed no significant relationship for activities and internality when the outcome was years of education. Activities did have a 5% relationship with job status—it was the second of two primary variables in the initial unconstrained analysis. For females, number of activities was related to years of education (7.7%), but this was substantially less than the 13.1% associated with educational expectation and a self-rating of ability for college, which were the primary predictors. Relationships were modest for internality in predicting job status for females. In no case for either form or sex were these variables related to income.

Conclusion. Generally, then, Underachievers who have relatively higher levels of self-esteem, who participate in activities, and who have an internal locus of control are more likely to have better educational and occupational outcomes than Underachieving students who do not; some of these factors are partly reflected in grade point average and measures of educational expectation and parental education which predict the criteria more efficiently. It must be pointed out, however, that although educational expectation and parental education subsume these variables and predict the outcome measures more strongly, self-esteem, activities, and internality may still be important functional expressions of these relationships. Such psychological dispositions are likely operating, but they may be only a few of the several factors indexed by educational expectation and parental education.

More interpretively, those Underachievers who have high perceived competence—who value education highly, expect to go on to college and obtain a good job, participate in activities, are reasonably self-confident, and have good self-esteem—do relatively better educationally and occupationally in the 13 years following high school. Conversely, Underachievers who have low perceived competence— are defeated by their underachievement, have low expectations and aspirations for their futures, do not participate in activities, seriously question their competence, and lack self-esteem—are less likely to do well educationally or occupationally after high school.

Do Underachievers Catch Up?

The above analyses were conducted within the Underachievement group alone, and they showed that some Underachievers do relatively better educationally and occupationally after high school than others. But how well do they do relative to what might have been expected had they not been Underachievers? Do they ever catch up educationally or occupationally to what would be predicted on the basis of their ability?

ANALYSIS STRATEGY

The analysis procedure was unusual. The question was whether the particular Underachievers with the best chance to do well (i.e., possessed characteristics found to forecast educational and occupational success) actually catch up to the educational and occupational levels of students in the comparison groups, especially the Same MA group. Because the previous regression analyses showed that two variables (e.g., educational expectation, midparent education) predicted outcome most efficiently for Underachievers for most sex and form samples, we determined high, medium, and low categories for each of these two variables such that 20%-30% of the Underachievers were classified into the two extreme categories. Then subjects in the other two groups (Same MA, Same GPA) were categorized by the same criteria.

These two classification schemes were the independent variables in analyses of covariance conducted separately for the Underachievers, Same MA, and Same GPA groups with years of education as the dependent variable and adjusted GPA as the covariate. This strategy "equated" the high, medium, and low groups on the predictors (e.g., educational expectation, mid-parent education) for high school GPA, but it did not adjust any differences between Underachievers and Same MA (selected to have higher grades) or between Underachievers and Same GPA (selected to be comparable in grades). Results were not materially different when Selected Underachievers were used, so they will not be discussed further. Overachievers were not analyzed.

The basic analyses, then, were Predictor 1 (e.g., high, medium, low educational expectation) × Predictor 2 (e.g., high, medium, low midparent education) analyses of covariance on years of education or on job status with adjusted GPA as the covariate, performed separately on the Underachievers, Same MA, and Same GPA groups. Which one or two predictors were used for which sex and form combinations were those major predictors listed in Table 7.1, although it must be remembered these were not independent of other predictors.

Essentially no interactions were found between the two predictors, so only main effects were estimated for each of the two predictor factors. Then on the same graph, the estimated effects (plus the grand mean) were plotted for the low-low, medium-medium, and high-high cells for the Underachievers, Same MA, and Same GPA groups. These plots permitted a visual determination of whether the differences between the Underachievers and the two comparison groups were parallel across levels of the two predictors or whether these groups converged as a function of these predictors (i.e., some Underachievers catch up).

As one looks at the graphs, one expects a general trend in which the outcome variable (e.g., years of education) increases from a low point for those subjects who were categorized as low-low on both the predictor variables (e.g., educational expectation, midparent education), through those classified as medium-medium, to a high point for those classified as high-high. This would simply reflect the already established predictive nature of these variables. We were more interested in the differences in slopes for these lines as a function of group. For example, if the lines for Same MA, Same GPA, and Underachievers all had the same slope with the Same MA a constant higher, then we would conclude that no subset of Underachievers catches up to what their abilities would predict (i.e., Same MA). But if the slopes were different, and the high-high Underachievers attained years of education equivalent to the high-high Same MA group, then we would conclude that those Underachievers with high educational expectations and high midparent education do catch up.

YEARS OF EDUCATION

The results for years of education are presented in figures 7.1 through 7.4 for males and females in Forms A and B. These graphs show the years of education, adjusted for GPA within groups, for students in the low-low, medium-medium, and high-high cells of the matrix of low-medium-high levels of the two best predictors of years

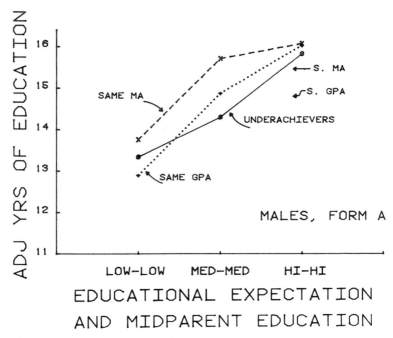

Figure 7.1. Adjusted years of education for low-low, medium-medium, and high-high educational expectation and midparent education subgroups within Underachievers, Same MA, and Same GPA comparison groups for Form A males

of education, plotted separately for the Underachievers, Same MA, and Same GPA groups. The points at the right labeled "S. MA" and "S. GPA" indicate the means of the Same MA and Same GPA groups across levels of the predictors.

Form A. The graphs for Form A show that the high-high Underachievers generally do better than the average of the other groups. Some Underachievers do catch up to what one would predict on the basis of their abilities (i.e., Same MA). For males (Figure 7.1), Underachievers with high educational expectations and high mid-parent education levels ultimately achieve as many years of education as they would have if they had not been Underachievers, but had these

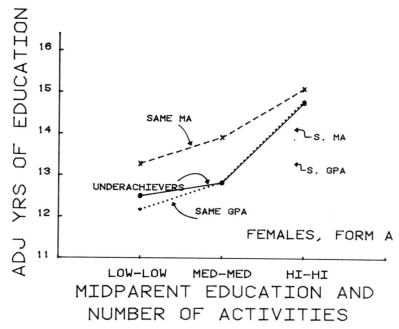

Figure 7.2. Adjusted years of education for low-low, medium-medium, and high-high midparent education and number of activities subgroups within Underachievers, Same MA, and Same GPA comparison groups for Form A females

same characteristics (i.e., comparably high educational expectations and mid-parent educations).

For the females (Figure 7.2), mid-parent education and number of activities were the principal predictors, and again the groups converge for those subjects with high levels on both these predictors.

Therefore, for Form A, some Underachievers do recover following high school and achieve the same number of years of education as would be expected if they had not been underachieving high school students.

Form B. The results for Form B did not conform to this conclusion. Males who were not Underachievers, but had the same mental ability (Same MA) completed more years of education (from 1.25 to 1.93

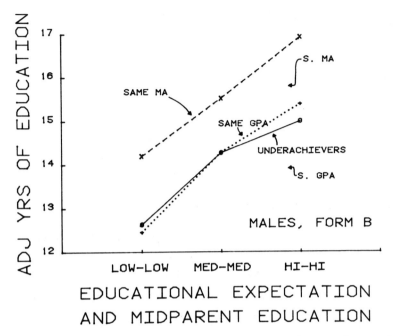

Figure 7.3. Adjusted years of education for low-low, medium-medium, and high-high educational expectation and midparent education subgroups within Underachievers, Same MA, and Same GPA comparison groups for Form B males

years) than Underachievers (Figure 7.3). Underachievers completed as many years of education as students with the same grades, but lower mental ability (Same GPA), and this was true regardless of the level of educational expectation or parent education. Stated another way, educational expectation and mid-parent education were related to number of years of education within each of the three groups, but high levels for these characteristics did not narrow the gap between Underachievers and the comparison groups.

For Form B females (Figure 7.4), educational expectation and the student's perceived ability to complete college were related to years of education within each group, but the three groups did not differ from one another, principally because the Same MA control group did not achieve as many years of education as in Form A.

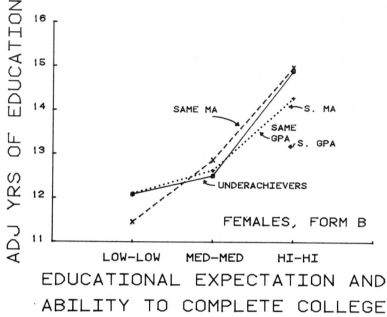

Figure 7.4. Adjusted years of education for low-low, medium-medium, and high-high educational expectation and ability to complete college subgroups within Underachievers, Same MA, and Same GPA comparison groups for Form B females

Conclusion. It is reasonable to conclude that underachievers who value education highly, participate in a number of activities, perceive themselves capable of completing college, and have parents with high levels of education do achieve more years of education than other underachievers. Moreover, some complete as many years of education as they would have if they had not been underachievers in high school. But high valuation of education, perceived competence, and self-confidence do not always lead to "complete" educational recovery.

CURRENT JOB STATUS

The trend for job status was similar for males in Forms A and B, and the results are pictured in figures 7.5 and 7.6. In both cases, the gap

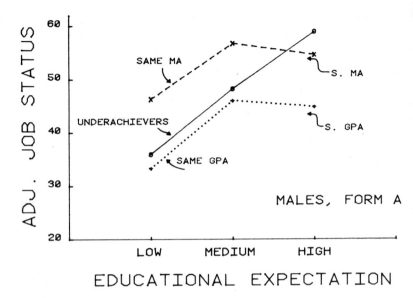

Figure 7.5. Adjusted job status for low, medium, and high educational expectation subgroups within Underachievers, Same MA, and Same GPA comparison groups for Form A males

for job status between underachievers and the Same MA group closes for students with high levels on the predictors.

Males. For Form A, the single predictor is educational expectation. For Form B, the two predictors are occupational aspirations and number of activities. Although the specific predictors differ between forms, the general result is the same: Male Underachievers who had high educational expectations or who had high occupational aspirations and participated in a great many school activities obtained jobs with social status comparable to those for students with the same mental ability who were not Underachievers (Same MA) and better than students with the same grades but lower mental ability (Same GPA).

Females. Predictions to job status for females were much weaker than for males. Occupational aspirations predicted modestly for Form

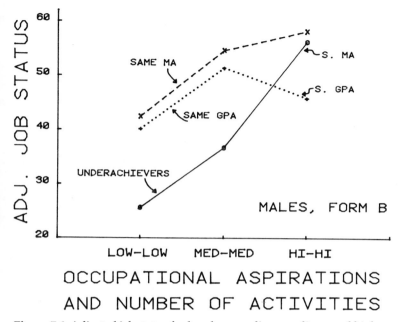

Figure 7.6. Adjusted job status for low-low, medium-medium, and high-high occupational aspirations and number of activities subgroups within Underachievers, Same MA, and Same GPA comparison groups for Form B males

A females, but no significant predictors were found for Form B females. As can be seen in Figure 7.7, Underachieving females with high levels of occupational aspirations obtained jobs with higher status than Underachievers with low occupational aspirations, but the gap between Underachievers and students with the same mental abilities did not narrow.

CURRENT JOB INCOME

No strong, consistent predictors of current job income were found, so further analyses were not conducted for this outcome measure. Recall, however, that at their first job and at their current job, Underachievers as a group earned less than the Same MA group and they progressed economically more slowly following their first job. As a

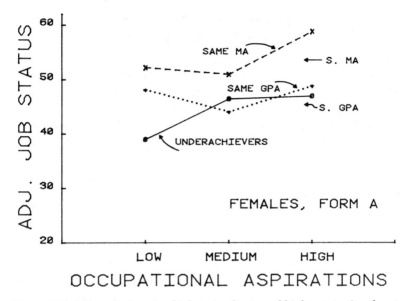

Figure 7.7. Adjusted job status for low, medium, and high occupational aspirations subgroups within Underachievers, Same MA, and Same GPA comparison groups for Form A females

group, then, Underachievers do not catch up economically. Some individuals, of course, do catch up, but we cannot predict who those individuals are from our research.

CONCLUSION

The results suggest that under some circumstances, underachieving students who value education and have families that support that value, who have participated in school activities and feel confident about completing college can often achieve as many years of education and obtain jobs with levels of status as high as students with those same characteristics who were not Underachievers in high school. Unfortunately, this result was not totally consistent across sex or form, so it would seem that other factors not specified here can mediate this relationship. Thus, it is possible for some Underachievers to "recover completely," but not all do so.

Level of Mental Ability and
Degree of Underachievement

One unique feature of our study is that we considered Underachievers across the entire range of mental ability. Much previous study focused on gifted Underachievers, so little attention has been paid to the level of mental ability among Underachievers, especially as a predictor of educational and occupational outcome. Most studies simply designate a child as an Underachiever by some criterion, but do not investigate degrees of underachievement. In this section we examine both these variables.

CORRELATIONAL ANALYSES

Table 7.2 presents the correlations and partial correlations controlling for adjusted grade point average between mental ability and degree of underachievement as predictors of educational and occupational outcome. The data are based only on Underachievers. The degree of underachievement is the residual from the regression of adjusted grade point average on mental ability, with the scale reversed so that high positive values reflect greater degrees of underachievement. Consequently, a large negative correlation means that the more serious the underachievement the less well a student does on the outcome variable.

Mental ability. As one would expect, the simple correlations between mental ability and attained years of education at the top of Table 7.2 are significant and range from .19 to .36. Correlations between mental ability and job status are significant for males, and correlations between mental ability and income are significant for females. Once adjusted grade point average is partialed out, however, no correlation is significant for males and those correlations that are significant for females are not replicated across forms. The correlations between mental ability and the covariate of adjusted grade average were .74 to .85.

These results seem to indicate that grade point average, not mental ability, is the most important predictor of educational and occu-

TABLE 7.2 Correlations and partial correlations (controlling adjusted GPA) for mental ability and degree of underachievement with educational and occupational outcome for Underachievers

	Years Education		Job Status		Income	
	Form A	Form B	Form A	Form B	Form A	Form B
Mental Ability						
Males						
Simple *r*:	.36***	.19*	.17*	.26***	−.03	.06
Partial *r*:	.00	−.08	−.11	.07	−.09	.07
Females						
Simple *r*:	.36***	.25**	.14	.14	.33***	.43***
Partial *r*:	.22*	−.06	.13	−.17	.28**	.14
Degree of Underachievement+						
Males						
Simple *r*:	−.13	−.21**	−.17*	−.07	−.09	.05
Partial *r*:	.00	−.08	−.10	.06	−.09	.06
Females						
Simple *r*:	.09	−.20*	.09	−.26**	.16	−.07
Partial *r*:	.22*	−.06	.13	−.15	.25**	.16

*, **, *** = $p < .05, .01, .001$
+A negative *r* means the more serious the underachievement the less well one does on the outcome variable.

pational outcome. This interpretation is bolstered by reversing the partialing variables and calculating the correlations between adjusted grade point average and the educational and occupational outcome variables with mental ability partialed out. When this is done, the simple correlations between grade point average and the outcome variables are somewhat higher and more consistent than those presented in Table 7.2 for males and about the same for females. Further, six of the eight correlations are still significant when mental ability is partialed out (in contrast to only two of eight remaining significant when grades are partialed out of the prediction from mental ability). Therefore, grade point average, as opposed to mental ability, is the more significant predictor of outcome among Underachievers.

Degree of underachievement. The bottom of Table 7.2 presents the correlations between the degree of underachievement and the educational and occupational outcome variables for Underachievers, either as simple correlations or as partial correlations with adjusted grade point average regressed out. Recall that a negative correlation means the more serious the underachievement the poorer the outcome.

For males, these simple relationships are modest and disappear entirely when grades are partialed out. For females, the results are quite inconsistent across form, to the point of analogous correlations having opposite signs.

Conclusion. In general, among Underachievers across sex and form, no obvious consistent relation exists between level of mental ability or degree of underachievement and educational or occupational outcome with or without covarying grades. Note that a relation does exist for males and females in both forms between mental ability and years of education, as well as between mental ability and job status (males only) and income (females only). But none of these relations survives for both forms after high school grades are partialed out, although grades still predict outcome after mental ability is partialed out. Therefore, from the standpoint of an underachieving child's educational and occupational future, mental ability is already reflected in his or her grades, as bad as they may seem, and will not necessarily contribute to future attainments over and above current grades.

INTERACTION ANALYSES

The analyses discussed above focus on linear and additive relations and are less sensitive to curvilinear or interactive relations. Therefore, we trichotomized the variables level of mental ability and degree of underachievement and analyzed them in the same way as the predictors of outcome described at the beginning of the section entitled "Do Underachievers Catch Up?"

The results are presented for years of education in Figure 7.8 for males and Figure 7.9 for females and for job status in Figure 7.10 for males. Main effects or interactions were not significant for other sex and outcome variable combinations. Although clearer for males, the major trend was consistent: If a youth seriously underachieves—more than approximately two grade levels—mental ability is irrelevant to

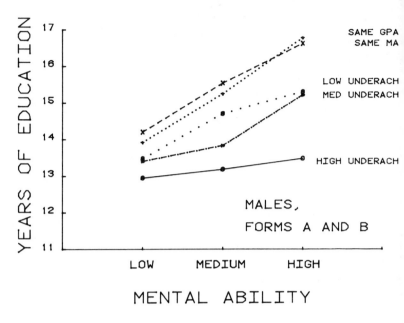

Figure 7.8. Years of education for low, medium, and high (severe) Under-achievers as a function of low, medium, and high mental ability in comparison with low, medium, and high mental ability subgroups of the Same MA and Same GPA comparison groups for Form A and B males

educational and occupational outcome. This means that youths with medium and high mental ability who seriously underachieve never recover. In fact, they attain educational and occupational levels only comparable to or below individuals with the lowest mental ability levels whether they were Underachievers or not.

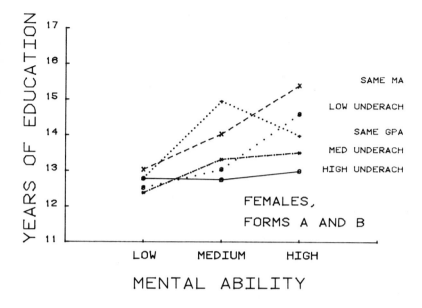

SAME MA

LOW UNDERACH

SAME GPA

MED UNDERACH

HIGH UNDERACH

FEMALES,
FORMS A AND B

Figure 7.9. Years of education for low, medium, and high (severe) Under-achievers as a function of low, medium, and high mental ability subgroups of the Same MA and Same GPA comparison groups for Form A and B females

Note

1. Robert B. McCall, Director, Office of Child Development, 2017 Cathedral of Learning, University of Pittsburgh, Pittsburgh, PA 15260.

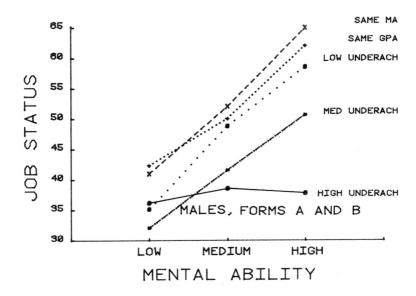

Figure 7.10. Job status for low, medium, and high (severe) Underachievers as a function of low, medium, and high mental ability in comparison with low, medium, and high mental ability subgroups of the Same MA and Same GPA comparison groups for Form A and B males

8

Conclusions and Implications

I n this section, we will summarize our major findings, integrate them with the previous literature,
and then discuss the conceptual and practical implications of our
work. Much previous study used specialized samples (e.g., children
with high IQs) and idiosyncratic definitions of underachievement. We
investigated underachievement across the entire range of ability in a
highly representative sample using what is becoming a more standard
definition of underachievement. Thus, our work has the potential of
resolving many of the inconsistencies in the literature regarding correlates of underachievement. Moreover, our results have implications
for determining whether underachievement is a unique syndrome
and a temporary or more long-term problem.

Summary and Integration
With Previous Literature

Results for contemporary relationships will be presented first, followed by long-term outcomes.

THE DEMOGRAPHICS OF UNDERACHIEVEMENT
IN HIGH SCHOOL

Sex ratio. When underachievers who span the entire spectrum of abilities were defined by a negative deviation of one standard error below the regression line of grades on mental ability, approximately twice as many males (2.17) were classified as underachievers as females.

The greater prevalence of male underachievers is consistent with the previous literature. Although the ratio might be expected to vary with the ability levels of the sample, twice as many males as females is not inconsistent with findings from other studies using special-ability samples, and it probably represents the minimum sex difference likely to be observed, because males are disproportionately represented in the extremes of the IQ and grades distributions.

The issue is why the sex difference exists. As discussed previously, because males are disproportionately represented in the extremes of IQ and school performance, a mean sex difference in the performance measure alone—.49 standardized grade units to be precise—would produce a 2:1 male to female ratio of underachievers using the regression definition. The mean sex difference in standardized grades (grades were standardized across, not within, sexes in the present study) was .36, and therefore almost three-fourths of the sex difference ratio observed here is associated with the average difference in grades between the sexes.

But it would be wrong psychologically to conclude that the sex ratio is artifactual. Grades are not issued separately within sexes, and students do not evaluate their performance relative to their sex. Any attributes that characterize male underachievers are likely to be no less real psychologically than if the sex ratio were not associated with mean differences in grades. Further, the correlates and consequences of underachievement were very similar for males and females, suggesting that underachievement is not fact for one sex and artifact for the other.

It could be argued, however, that given the 2:1 ratio, the group of girls designated as underachievers were more extreme than the group of boys so classified. As a result, the characteristics and correlates for girls might be weaker or qualitatively different if underachievement were defined separately within sex. There is validity to this point and potential to its implications, but it and the artifactual sex ratio issue both rest on the same perspective. They are valid if one assumes that underachievement is different for the sexes and should be defined separately within each sex. Conversely, they are not obviously valid if one assumes that the natural context of schooling does not typically distinguish and treat males and females separately and that the parents, teachers, and youths do not adjust their perceptions of expected performance as a function of sex. We tend to side with the latter perspective.

Socioeconomic status. In our study, underachievers came from all socioeconomic classes. There was a tendency for them to come from lower levels in Form B, but this was not replicated in Form A.

It is often concluded in the literature that underachievers come disproportionately from lower socioeconomic classes. Some empirical studies find this to be true, but others do not (paralleling the inconsistent results for forms A and B), and most studies lack appropriate comparison groups. Undoubtedly, the relation depends partly on how underachievers are sampled and defined. If they are defined to be of relatively high mental ability or are taken from special programs or clinic groups composed of students placed by their parents, they are likely to come from the middle and upper-middle classes. When a broader spectrum of abilities is sampled and the regression definition is used, underachievers may not differ in SES from other students. Indeed, one of the advantages of the regression definition is that, in contrast to other definitions, it is more likely to designate as underachievers a group that is not different in ability from the total sample.

Race. We observed no differences in the racial distribution of underachievers relative to comparison groups. Race has not been examined systematically heretofore, and our results may not generalize to samples in locales or times with racial and ethnic compositions different from those in the state of Washington between 1965 and 1980. It should be remembered that only 2% of the total follow-up sample on which we based our study was nonwhite.

Birth order. Similarly, no consistent differences were observed for birth order, although Form B underachieving females were more likely to be later born.

It is often claimed in the clinical literature that underachievers tend to be later born with very achieving older siblings, but empirically this has not been consistently found. If this difference exists in clinic populations, it may be a function of parental SES or even a contrast effect in which a parent is more likely to be concerned and seek help when there is a substantial difference in the achievement levels of siblings, especially if the firstborn child sets a high standard of achievement for subsequent children. If this speculation is true, one might expect a birth order effect in high-education or high-ability or in clinic samples.

Family size. No differences were observed for family size, although a few studies in the literature indicate underachievers tend to come from larger families. Those same studies also tend to show them to come from lower socioeconomic classes, and it is likely that low SES and large family size are correlated in such samples. Again, family size as well as SES may be variables in selected samples, but not when underachievement is defined across the entire range of abilities.

Size of town. Underachievers came from both large and small cities. They were more likely to come from big cities in Form A, but more likely to live in the country in Form B.

A few studies in the literature seem to suggest underachievers come from small towns, but our more broadly based sample reveals no consistent pattern in this regard.

Working mothers. No consistent differences occurred in the likelihood of the mothers of underachievers being employed outside the home, although female underachievers in Form A were *less*, not more, likely to have mothers that worked. Therefore, even for a time when working mothers were relatively unusual, no consistent differences were found.

The previous literature was similarly inconsistent. Because the likelihood of mothers working has increased dramatically in recent years, one cannot generalize these results to contemporary circumstances.

Divorce. No differences were observed for the divorce rates of parents, although the literature frequently asserts that single-parent families are disproportionately represented among underachievers. Again, divorce may be more common among underachievers of higher ability, but not across the broad range of abilities. Recent changes in the frequency and nature of divorce may limit generalizations from these data to contemporary circumstances.

PERSONAL CHARACTERISTICS OF UNDERACHIEVERS

Self-perception. Relative to students of the same ability, underachievers consistently had substantially poorer self-concepts. Underachievers had lower perceptions of their current and future educational abilities, general competence, and self-esteem, as well as lower educational and occupational aspirations and expectations.

The literature emphasizes the lower self-perceptions of underachievers, especially their lower self-esteem. These themes were borne out in our study, which included a more systematic comparison between underachievers and achieving students with the same mental ability. Self-esteem and self-perceptions did not strongly or consistently distinguish underachievers from non-underachieving students with the same grades, however. Therefore, poor self-perceptions seem to be more strongly associated with grade level than with underachievement per se, a finding consistent with the proposition that school performance is more likely to produce self-perceptions than to follow from them (e.g., Alexander & Eckland, 1975).

Goal orientation. As indicated above, underachievers had markedly lower educational and occupational aspirations and expectations, consistent with the literature. Also, underachievers of both sexes had thought less about their future careers. These contrasts were more marked when compared to the same MA than to same GPA groups.

Peer relations. Underachievers tended to participate less in activities and to hold fewer offices in extracurricular activity groups, but female underachievers claimed to have more friends than comparison students. Underachievers of both sexes tended to date more extensively and have more intense heterosexual relations, but social factors seemed to be stronger correlates for females than for males.

The literature frequently indicates that underachievers have poor social skills and few friends and tend to be either aggressive or shy and withdrawn. It is also acknowledged, however, that some underachievers are quite socially skilled. The net effect of these different characteristics may be that underachievers cannot be characterized easily as a single group with respect to peer relations. The more intense and frequent heterosexual relations by underachievers might be a consequence of few friends and poor self-esteem producing the need for the social support and security that intimate relations sometimes offer. This pattern may also foreshadow higher divorce rates (see below).

Parental relations. Although no significant differences were observed for a composite measure of parental closeness, underachieving males tended to have either very close or very distant relationships with their parents. Such extreme relationships were more likely for males than females, and if any differences existed for females, these consisted of more distant relationships with parents.

The clinical literature on underachievement suggests that some underachievers have been made dependent by overly helpful parents. Some of these children may remain shy, withdrawn, and overtly dependent; others may rebel, superficially strive for independence, and become aggressive or hostile. Our data are not strong in this regard and more definitive for males than females, but comport with this clinical interpretation that both extremes are possible.

Locus of control. Underachievers showed no differences in locus of control. Although the previous literature indicates that underachievers tend to have an external locus of control, this often consists of blaming other people for their problems. This characteristic may not generalize to the other contexts in which this variable was measured here.

Counselors' judgment. Counselors, when asked if a student in our sample was an underachiever, correctly detected only half of the underachievers defined in the current study (they were even worse at identifying overachievers, especially among females). Approximately the same percentage of underachievers were identified by teachers in a study using a different type of sample and definition of under-achievement (Carr et al., 1991).

Counselors presumably have access to grades and test scores, but it does not appear that they rely on such information to a great extent. Students who come from less advantageous home surroundings, but who test well, may not be perceived as underachievers. In any event, the accuracy levels are not good, and schools desiring to implement programs for underachievers are advised to rely on objective assessments rather than counselors' judgments.

Types of underachievers. An attempt to cluster underachievers into types or syndromes failed to produce a few groups of underachievers with clear-cut characteristics. This outcome may result from under-achievers being a very heterogeneous group, especially when all ability levels are represented, or the particular variables used in the clustering attempts not accurately reflecting the dimensions along which types or syndromes of underachievement are characterized. For example, no measures of aggressive/rebellious versus shy/compliant were available for the clustering analysis.

Mental ability or grades. All of the above personal characteristics predominantly distinguish underachievers from students with the same mental ability whose grades were higher and concordant with what would be expected on the basis of their ability test scores. These characteristics contrast underachievers with what might have been expected if the students had not been underachievers. However, one can also ask whether underachievers are different from students with the same grades but lower mental ability. Our data clearly demonstrated that underachievers were essentially no different in their demographic, personal, and social characteristics than non-underachieving students with the same grades. Viewed another way, the study revealed no consistent characteristics during high school associated uniquely with *under*achievement per se, only with relatively poorer school achievement.

Although giving this as the broad conclusion, we must acknowledge that it was not always true. For some comparisons, underachievers had lower assessments of their current schoolwork and their educational and occupational futures, they engaged in fewer extracurricular activities, and they sometimes had more intense and advanced heterosexual relations than non-underachieving youths with the same grades. Although these characteristics did not replicate across form and sex, they gain some interpretive credibility because they foreshadow the long-term consequences that do consistently relate to underachievement per se.

THE LONG-TERM EDUCATIONAL AND OCCUPATIONAL PROGNOSIS

First job. Underachievers did not attain a first job commensurate in status or income with their mental ability. Instead, their first employment was consistent with other students who had the same high school grades. This result is not surprising, because a primary basis for obtaining first employment is school performance.

Attained education. Underachievers completed fewer years of postsecondary education than achievers of the same mental ability, and they were less likely to complete college than *either* comparison group. Underachieving males completed 1.63 years of formal education (10.5%) less and underachieving females completed 1.05 years of education (7.4%) less than achieving students of the same ability.

Further, male underachievers were almost twice as likely to go to a vocational or technical school, more than one-third as likely to attend a professional school, about as likely to attend a junior or community college, but only one-half as likely to attend a college or university than achieving students of the same ability. Of those who did attend a college or university, twice as many male underachievers dropped out and only half as many graduated.

The results for underachieving females were similar, but the magnitude of differences were not as great. Underachieving females were 57% more likely to go to vocational or technical school, about as likely to go to junior or community college, and only 42% as likely to attend a college or university. Of those who did attend a college or university, underachieving females were 42% more likely to drop out before graduation.

Underachievers of both sexes were less likely to complete college. For the sexes combined, underachievers had only one chance in five of completing 4 years of college, whereas the achieving student of comparable mental ability had better than one chance in two of completing college—a likelihood two and a half times greater. Moreover, underachievers were somewhat less likely to complete college than young people with the same high school grades, the latter group having a one-third greater likelihood of completing 4 years of college than underachievers. Completing college, then, was one characteristic unique to underachievement and not due simply to poorer grades.

Occupational status. Thirteen years after high school, underachievers held jobs of lower status than achieving students of the same mental ability, but the average status was the same as for students with comparable high school grades who were not underachievers. The measurement scales do not permit percentile comparisons.

Income. Underachievers earned less money 13 years after high school than did achieving students of the same ability. Underachieving males earned $.76 (7.7%) less per hour and underachieving females earned $.73 (12.2%) less per hour than achieving students of the same ability. But underachievers made the same incomes as achieving students with the same high school grades.

Bad start or persistent underachievement? Underachievers not only get off to a poorer start in the job market, but do not progress as fast thereafter. Analyses of covariance using the status and income of the first job as covariates showed that differences in education and status and income of jobs 13 years after high school were still lower for underachievers relative to achieving students with the same mental ability.

Number of jobs. There was a slight tendency for underachievers to hold more jobs during the 13 years after high school relative to achieving students of the same mental ability and to students with the same grades. Although this latter result was not statistically consistent for all comparisons, frequent job changes may also be a unique characteristic of underachievement.

Military service. Male underachievers were 50% more likely to enter the military than achieving students with the same mental ability, but rates were similar for students with the same grades.

Divorce. Underachievers were 50% more likely to divorce in the 13 years following high school than either of the other comparison groups. Although the trend was more emphatic for females, with underachieving females having a divorce rate of 51% (twice that of underachieving males), the group differences were consistent in relative magnitude for the two sexes. This is another clear demonstration that underachievers are at a disadvantage even with respect to students with the same grades. The higher divorce rates may also be associated with the earlier and more intense heterosexual relations that some underachievers displayed, perhaps leading to marriage at a more immature age and subsequent divorce.

Predictors of adult attainment for underachievers. Some underachievers attained more education and better jobs than others. Even after adjustments are made for grade point average, underachieving high school students who expected to go to college and to graduate, who believed they were sufficiently competent to complete college, who displayed relatively more interest in academic schoolwork, who participated in school and nonschool activities, who had relatively more self-esteem and self-confidence, and who had parents who were relatively more educated did better educationally and occupationally 13 years after high school. This collection of characteristics was best indexed by the student's educational expectation and the parents' education level. Note that these are some of the same high school variables that generally distinguished underachievers as a group from achieving students with the same mental ability.

It may be that some students underachieve because of a temporary lack of commitment to school—perhaps because they are emphasizing other activities or preoccupied with having a good social time. If they value education highly and hold some degree of perceived competence, self-confidence, and expectation to pursue and complete their education, they ultimately do better.

Relatively few variables predicted income.

Do underachievers catch up? Some underachievers with high educational or occupational aspirations and expectations and highly educated parents ultimately did catch up educationally and occupationally to achieving students of the same mental ability. This was not uniformly the case, because it was not consistently replicated across forms. Moreover, underachievers whose grades were substantially below expectations (e.g., two or more grade levels) did not catch up, and they only attained educational and occupational levels comparable to students with the worst ability levels and grades. This result implies that severe underachievement is worse in terms of educational and occupational success than poor grades for those youths with medium and especially high mental ability.

Therefore, the often-heard comments of teachers and others consoling parents with the assertion than an underachiever will ultimately "get his or her act together" after leaving high school and the family nest is partly true. But not all underachievers ultimately attain education and employment consistent with their abilities—in fact, relatively small percentages do. If a youngster is underachieving by only a grade or so; comes from highly educated parents; and possesses the aspirations, expectations, and self-confidence for attainment, then complete catching up is possible, but not assured. Otherwise, it seems, under-achievement is a relatively permanent characteristic.

Conceptual and
Methodological Implications

These data have implications for understanding the nature of un-derachievement and for taking action.

IS UNDERACHIEVEMENT A SYNDROME?

Underachievers differed in many ways from achieving students with the same mental ability, but for the most part they were very similar to students who had the same grades but were not under-achieving. Our study is perhaps the first to make a systematic com-parison between underachievers and same-grade controls on such a broad spectrum of measures, and the failure to find systematic and consistent differences between these groups appears *in its unqualified version* to have major implications for the validity of the concept of underachievement.

For one thing, this unqualified result alleges that many of the characteristics in the clinical and counseling literature typically attrib-uted to underachievers are actually more likely to be associated with low achievement (i.e., grades) than underachievement per se. Could it be that no unique clinical syndrome of underachievement exists?

Further, if taken on its face and without qualifications, the conclu-sion would seem to be that grades are everything and ability (after grades) is nothing. Indeed, the sociological literature on general status attainment (i.e., educational and occupational achievement) is quite consistent with this proposition, finding that grades in high school embody most of the variance in predicting future outcome associated with ability, family socioeconomic status, and perceived competence (e.g., Alexander & Eckland, 1975; Featherman, 1980; Sewell, Hauser, & Wolf, 1980). Two additional implications would follow from this. First, either assessing mental ability is of limited utility and/or the measure of mental ability used in this study is of limited validity for this purpose. Second, although underachievement is prediction error from one standpoint, it is simply one portion of the grade distribution from another standpoint, and therefore one should expect under-achievers and the role of grades to fit with the broader literature on achievement. This proposition, apparently supported in retrospect, was not obvious before this study. Indeed, underachievers, by defi-nition, are exceptions to the main ability-grades relation, and there-fore, underachievers might be expected to be exceptions to the pattern of relations previously found for grades and the grades-ability combination.

Evidence for a syndrome. The general thrust of the results favored the proposition that underachievers were very similar to non-under-achieving youths with the same grades, but we found exceptions to this general pattern. Those exceptions have a conceptual theme that makes sense, and they demonstrate that characteristics exist that are unique in degree to underachievers, not just low achievers.

Underachievers were less likely to complete 4 years of college, were more likely to divorce, and were likely to change jobs more frequently than comparison students with the same grades but somewhat lower mental ability. Also, although not uniform across all groups and comparisons, during high school, underachievers had lower assess-ments of their current schoolwork and their educational and occupa-tional futures, they participated less in extracurricular activities, and they were involved in more advanced and intense heterosexual rela-tionships than same-grade controls.

Failure to persist. At a strictly behavioral level, the failure to com-plete college, sustain a marriage, and retain a job all suggest that *underachievers lack persistence in the face of challenge and adversity.* High school academics, college, employment, and marriage all require some self-confidence and the ability to continue when the going becomes difficult. Underachievers do not persist in these activities as long as others with either the same mental ability or the same grades. Instead of persevering and attempting to conquer the inevi-table difficulties of life, they check out. They lack "stick-to-itiveness" (U. Bronfenbrenner, personal communication, 1991).

So, underachievers do exhibit a behavioral theme unique in degree to them that defines their syndrome—the inability to persist in the face of challenge—and which apparently persists at least for the next 13 years.

Severe underachievement. A second unique theme was that severe underachievement, in which school performance was two or more grades below expectation, was more devastating in the long run for youths of medium and especially those who have high ability than for less severely underachieving youths regardless of grade level. Such extreme cases performed educationally and occupationally at levels equivalent to youths with the lowest levels of mental ability and grades. In many respects, these are the best minds wasted by underachievement.

Perceived competency. A third theme unique in degree to underachievers was more subtle. *Many underachievers may have lower perceived competency.* Although not always replicated across form, underachievers during high school sometimes had lower perceptions of their schoolwork and their educational and occupational futures, they sometimes participated less in extracurricular activities, and some had more advanced and intense heterosexual relations than non-underachieving youths with the same grades. Moreover, those underachievers who were less likely to catch up to what their abilities predict had lower educational and occupational aspirations and expectations, poorer self-esteem, less well-educated parents, and a stronger perception that external, rather than personal, factors controlled their lives than youths with the same grades.

Collectively, these characteristics suggest that underachievers have lower perceived competence relative to their grades, and perhaps as a consequence, they lack the disposition to persist at educational, occupational, and personal tasks in the face of challenge. Further, such a disposition persists at least for 13 years after high school and perhaps beyond.

At least one study in the literature potentially supports such a long-term conclusion. Although not concerned with underachievers per se, Clausen (1991) defined "planful competence," measured in adolescence, to be similar to Smith's (1968) conception of competence in Peace Corps volunteers (e.g., self-respect, feelings of efficacy, realistic goal setting, intelligence, and dependability). Clausen's planned competence was measured by three components, described here for the low end of the dimension, which is similar to characteristics of underachievers:

1. Lack of dependability (tends to be rebellious, self-defeating in regard to own goals, pushes limits, sees what he/she can get away with)
2. Intellectually uninvested (uncomfortable with uncertainty and complexity; conventional and conforming; disorganized and maladaptive under stress or trauma; has a small reserve of integration)
3. Victimized versus self-confident (self-pitying, feels cheated and victimized by life, behaves as if generally fearful in manner and approach, self-defeating)

Elements of the lack of self-esteem, the inability to interact positively with others, external locus of control, low expectations and aspirations, and failure to persist in the face of uncertainty and challenge uniquely characteristic of underachievers can be seen as similar to Clausen's lack of planned competence.

In Clausen's study, subjects were followed from adolescence to between 53 and 62 years of age. Adolescent planned competence forecast in adulthood educational attainment (better for males than parental SES or IQ), occupational attainment (for males only, but better than other variables), male career orderliness and stability (increasing status and few job changes that deviate from a definite career path), and (negatively) number of marriages (both sexes)—the same outcome variables we found to be uniquely associated in degree with underachievement. Although these data cannot replicate the uniqueness of underachievement, they do provide some support for the persistence well into adulthood of characteristics similar to those found here to be associated with underachievement.

METHODOLOGICAL ADVANTAGES AND LIMITATIONS

The current study contained several methodological advantages as well as limitations that should be kept in mind in interpreting the results.

Sample size. We used one of the largest samples of underachievers in the literature, and the ability to replicate some findings across subsamples (i.e., forms) is a rare strength.

Sample breadth. Ours is one of the few studies of underachievement that covers the entire range of abilities, enabling broad conclusions with a greater likelihood of being replicated, but accompanied by the liability of masking relations and effects that may exist for one subgroup or another. For example, it was speculated at the beginning that current interest focuses on underachieving students from educationally and financially poor circumstances and on underachieving students from advantaged homes who are not living up to the high standards of their parents. The dynamics and potential outcomes for these subgroups may be quite different. Indeed, it appears that underachievers with well-educated parents have a greater likelihood of "recovering" and achieving up to their abilities than do youths from less advantaged homes. Further, an underachiever from a poorly educated family may not be perceived by school personnel as underachieving his or her potential, but rather as testing unduly well. Therefore, important differences may characterize certain subgroups within this broad sample.

Age. The underachievers studied here were defined during high school. It is unlikely that the results observed also characterize the situation for younger children.

Confounding circumstances. Youths with learning disabilities, mental or physical handicaps, and other specific disorders or limitations were not isolated in this study as they would be in today's educational situation. On the positive side, underachievement may or may not characterize such special students, and the current study includes as underachievers all who qualify regardless of reason. On the negative side, the generality of the findings to contemporary education is compromised somewhat, because such students would be given special services and classified according to their disability, not as underachievers, despite the fact that underachievement is often one of the criteria for diagnosing a youth as having special needs.

The mental ability measure. One might argue that the measure of mental ability in this study was inappropriate. It had the distinct disadvantages of consisting of numerous different tests, not one instrument; the most frequently administered test was unique to the state of Washington, and the tests were group measures of aptitude and achievement, not "pure ability," such as IQ.

As discussed above, however, it is not clear just how much difference exists between IQ, aptitude, and achievement tests, and the observed pattern of correlations among different tests did not reveal obvious distinctions. From a practical standpoint, it would be impossible to individually administer over 6,720 IQ tests across 25 schools in an entire state. Indeed, much of the previous work on achievement and status attainment using large samples and similar data has relied on brief (20 items) unstandardized and unresearched ability measures (e.g., see Alexander & Eckland, 1975).

On the positive side, the current ability measures have more ecological validity than conceptually more ideal assessments. These tests are what schools used in the mid-1960s, and they are close to what schools use today. Indeed, had IQ tests been available and used, the results would have less direct relevance and application to practical screening and detection issues in schools today.

Sex differences. Underachievement was not defined separately for the two sexes, and it is likely that much of the 2:1 male to female ratio of underachievers is associated with the lower grades typically obtained by boys even though they have comparable test scores. But, of course, the tests often are deliberately composed of items that do not distinguish between the sexes, so one can wonder whether males and females actually have the same abilities. We further argue that males and females do not perceive or evaluate their academic performance relative to their sex, so underachievement, in fact, may not be equally distributed between the sexes.

It should be noted that all females were analyzed, regardless of whether they chose to work outside the home after high school. Many early studies of status attainment in large samples did not study females at all or only included those who attempted employment (e.g., see Alexander & Eckland, 1975). It is true that measures of educational and occupational attainment depend upon opportunity and women did not have the opportunity or social support in these pursuits that men had, but it is important to note that although the absolute values of some results were different for the sexes, the relative trends within a sex were remarkably similar for males and females.

Comparison groups. · Because of our definition of underachievement, the comparison groups were not perfectly matched. Nevertheless, the pattern of results over all types of comparisons was quite consistent in converging on the major conclusions, which insofar as possible, were not discordant with the available literature. Although no single comparison is "pure," we believe the convergence over several imperfect comparisons lends credence to the findings.

Practical and Policy Concerns

For all but a modest percentage, chronic high school underachievement is not a temporary condition. The overriding conclusion from our research is that most high school underachievers remain underachievers into adult life with respect to further education, job status, and even marriage. They begin their postsecondary educational and employment careers at a disadvantage relative to their abilities, they do not progress as rapidly in these pursuits thereafter, and 13 years after high school, most have achieved less than their presumed potential. These findings have several practical implications for parents and society as well as for education.

FOR PARENTS AND SOCIETY

More serious problem today. The underachievers in this study were chronic and persistent; stability of some unspecified degree is suspected to emerge for underachievers in early elementary school for boys and junior high school or early high school for girls (Shaw & McCuen, 1960). Grades were averaged over all 4 years of high school to define underachievers in this study, so it is likely that the under-achievers we studied, especially the boys, had long histories of poor school performance, and the sequelae of their underachievement are more likely to persist than for children who underachieve earlier in their school careers (who may recover before they leave high school). Nevertheless, with three exceptions, high school dropouts were not included in this sample. It was not much of a problem then. But the consequences of dropping out of high school are likely to be more severe and persistent than for underachieving and staying in school, and with today's much higher dropout rates, dropout underachievers may present a serious, long-term problem.

Will they get their acts together? School authorities often try to con-sole parents of underachievers by telling them that their youths will surprise them and "get their acts together" once they leave home. And, according to the present data, some do, especially those who, as high school students, expect to achieve, hold justifiably high percep-tions of self-competence, have highly educated parents, and are not underachieving more than approximately 1.5 to 2.0 grade points below expectancy. But this is not a large group, and not all of such students eventually achieve up to their potential. To be sure, it is possible for a youth to be a couch potato for 6 years after high school and then go to college and graduate school, but he or she still will be behind expectations 13 years after high school. Perhaps 13 years is not a sufficiently long follow-up period—but it is approximately 30% of one's working years, and Clausen's (1991) data suggest the effect might last into the 60s, including essentially all of one's working life.

Eye of the beholder. The main outcome variables in this study were attained education, job status, and income relative to individuals with the same mental ability or the same high school grades. Nearly all underachievers who wanted employment were employed, and our crude measure of job satisfaction showed they were no less satisfied with their jobs than comparison groups. One could argue that most underachievers are happy and productive adults who do not perceive themselves as underachieving. Perhaps they are only underachievers in the eyes of some of their parents and the psychologists who study them.

But their divorces and job shifts must either produce or result from some degree of personal stress, and in today's high-technology society built on the premise of education, it is difficult to disregard the saying that a mind—even part of one—is a terrible thing to waste. The devastating outcome for severe underachievers makes it plausible to believe that many of these individuals are anxious about their performance and their lives in a society that emphasizes educational and occupational success, perhaps beyond the limits of reasonable balance. It is hard for us to accept the proposition that most of these individuals are free of stress and that only their parents or society are concerned.

At the same time, we believe that for youths from well-educated families, part of the problem may be located in the beholder. Well-educated, high-status, financially successful parents and a good many striving middle-class parents embracing the Protestant ethic, believe that children should do as well, probably better, than their parents. To do less well is failure. But regression to the mean is not just a statistical abstraction—it happens in reality. And the greater the disparity between parent and child success, the greater the concern the parents feel.

Some adjustment of parental attitudes may be necessary. U.S. society holds a very narrow definition of achievement and success. Alternatives to formal education, job status, and financial success are not valued, except possibly if they are practiced at a world-class level; the arts, many social services, and good parenting come to mind as undervalued achievements. So one suggestion to parents of underachievers is to broaden their value system, adjust their expectations, and accept their children's skills for whatever they are.

FOR EDUCATION

Generally, most states (at least one exception is California), school systems, and individual schools do not systematically try to identify underachievers or provide special services for them.

Programs commonly exist for the retarded, the learning disabled, the physically handicapped, and even those who are behaviorally disruptive, and underperformance may be one of several criteria. But if a student's *only* problem is lack of motivation and underachievement, special help is typically not available. In fact, severely underachieving students may be moved to easier and easier courses until their minimal effort is sufficient to pass. The student learns that an easier way can always be found—in short, the system rewards lack of effort. It would seem that the futures of these youngsters and society are just as worthy of remediation and special help as other groups who do not perform well in school because of physical and neurological disorders.

Identification. It seems clear from the limited data presented here and elsewhere, that school counselors are not very accurate or complete at identifying underachievers. They identified only half the underachievers in the current study. A systematic, comprehensive, repeated, objective testing procedure would need to be established, perhaps in a two-stage process consisting of screening followed by more intense diagnosis for those found to be at risk. Although few data exist on age of onset or when underachievement becomes persistent, such identification procedures should probably begin at least by late elementary school. However, this procedure would certainly raise the old issue of accuracy and bias in testing.

Treatment. There is no sense in identifying underachievers unless the schools can offer effective remediation and treatment. Unfortunately, the literature on intervention and treatment, reviewed in chapter 3, is not encouraging. We would argue that few serious comprehensive interventions have been attempted, and that a good deal of research is needed before establishing a routine program. Otherwise, educational critics, who justifiably argue that most massive special education programs, such as Chapter 1, do not work for most students (Slavin, 1989), likely—and perhaps correctly—will squelch any new programs for different problems.

What kind of a serious, comprehensive treatment program should be explored? From a prevention standpoint, most of the proposals to turn poor schools around, which assume their poorly performing pupils could do better, are likely to be appropriate for preventing and treating underachievement as defined here. These programs consist of establishing a climate of expectancy for learning and performance; removing negative stigmata; requiring all pupils to pass a common core curriculum at a minimum level of competence; encouraging parent and student participation in school policies; insisting upon extra help and work during and after school; using curricula and methods of teaching that relate the material to practical life experiences; and providing an integrated, comprehensive, case-managed set of family services (Slavin, Karweit, & Madden, 1989). Modularized curricula, in which the material is broken down into small steps and students proceed at their own pace and are "graded" by the number of units passed at some minimum standard, also might be tried, especially for lower-ability underachievers.

The periodic progress report system has the most evidence supporting its effectiveness, and it would seem to be a reasonable first step. The major behavioral problem for underachievers is lack of persistence in the face of challenge and lack of perceived competence, self-esteem, and internal control. Behavioral approaches to rewarding persistence are certainly possible, and a step-by-step, modular curriculum would foster success experiences, which are far better at promoting self-esteem, feelings of competence, and internal control than directly teaching such attitudes (Dweck & Elliott, 1983). No comprehensive program based on these principles has been seriously tried and evaluated as a treatment for underachievers.

In serious cases, family intervention may be necessary, especially in cases in which the youth's underachievement has become a source of frustration and conflict in the family. If rebelliousness and conflict with parents over schoolwork is an issue, family therapy might succeed best if it is integrated with systematic school efforts to deal with school behavior and performance, removing this item from the parents' agenda.

Epilogue

What does this study say to the Landises, Chadwicks, and Latimers—the parents whose experiences are recounted in the prologue?

On the one hand, the message is depressing. Underachievers tend not to persist in the face of challenge, and this disposition will likely last many years, leading to less education, more frequent job changes, and riskier marriages than would be expected for individuals with similar abilities and even similar grades.

On the other hand, this prognosis is not inevitable. Some, especially those from better-educated families who have more self-confidence, do escape this outcome. In the meantime, many parents should try harder not to try so hard to help or push their children; they should seek professional help, adjust their hopes and expectancies for their children, love them "where they're at," and perhaps patiently encourage persistence in the face of difficulty. And perhaps such parents should join with educators and psychologists in recognizing that underachievement is a long-term problem and that we all must work together to explore ways to treat and prevent it for future generations.

References

Alexander, K. L., & Eckland, B. K. (1975). School experience and status attainment. In S. E. Dragastin & G. H. Elder, Jr. (Eds.), *Adolescence in the life cycle*. New York: John Wiley.

Annesley, F., Odhner, F., Madoff, E., & Chansky, N. (1970). Identifying the first grade underachiever. *Journal of Educational Research, 63,* 459-462.

Appelbaum, M. I., & McCall, R. B. (1983). Design and analysis in developmental psychology. In W. Kessen (Ed.), *Handbook of child psychology* (3rd ed., vol. 1, pp. 415-476). New York: John Wiley.

Asbury, C. A. (1974). Selected factors influencing over- and underachievement in young school-aged children. *Review of Educational Research, 44,* 409-428.

Atkeson, B. M., & Forehand, R. (1978). Parents as behavior change agents with school-related problems. *Education and Urban Society, 10,* 521-540.

Atkeson, B. M., & Forehand, R. (1979). Home-based reinforcement programs designed to modify classroom behavior: A review and methodological evaluation. *Psychological Bulletin, 86,* 1298-1308.

Barrett, H. O. (1957). An intensive study of 32 gifted children. *Personnel and Guidance Journal, 36,* 192-194.

Belcastro, F. P. (1985). Use of behavior modification with academically gifted students: A review of the research. *Roeper Review, 7,* 184-187.

Bish, C. E. (1963). Underachievement of gifted students. In L. D. Crow & A. Crow (Eds.), *Educating the academically able* (pp. 226-229). New York: David McKay.

Blau, P. M., & Duncan, O. D. (1967). *The American occupational structure*. New York: John Wiley.

Borkowski, J. G., Carr, M., Rellinger, E., & Pressley, M. (1990). Self-regulated cognition: Interdependence of meta cognition, attributions, and self-esteem. In B. Jones & L. Idol (Eds.), *Dimensions of thinking* (pp. 53-92). Hillsdale NJ: Erlbaum.

154

Bricklin, B., & Bricklin, P. M. (1967). *Bright child—poor grades: The psychology of under-achievement.* New York: Delacorte.

Broman, S., Bien, E., & Shaughnessy, P. (1985). *Low achieving children: The first seven years.* Hillsdale, NJ: Lawrence Erlbaum.

Bronfenbrenner, U. (1991). Personal communication.

Calhoun, S. R. (1956). The effect of counseling on a group of underachievers. *School Review, 64,* 312-316.

Carr, M., Borkowski, J. G., & Maxwell, S. E. (1991). Motivational components of underachievement. *Developmental Psychology, 27,* 108-118.

Clark, B. (1979). *Growing up gifted.* Columbus, OH: Charles E. Merrill.

Clausen, J. A. (1991). Adolescent competence and the shaping of the life course. *American Journal of Sociology, 96,* 805-842.

Combs, C. F. (1964). Perception of self and scholastic underachievement in the academically capable. *Personnel and Guidance Journal, 43,* 47-51.

Crittenden, M. R., Kaplan, M. H., & Heim, J. K. (1984). Developing effective study skills and self-confidence in academically able young adolescents. *Gifted Child Quarterly, 28,* 25-30.

Cronbach, L. J. (1990). *Essentials of psychological testing.* New York: Harper & Row.

Curry, R. L. (1961). Certain characteristics of underachievers and overachievers. *Peabody Journal of Education, 39,* 41-45.

Cutts, N. E., & Moseley, N. (1957). *Teaching the bright and gifted.* Englewood Cliffs, NJ: Prentice-Hall.

Davis, H. B., & Connell, J. P. (1985). The effect of aptitude and achievement status on the self-system. *Gifted Child Quarterly, 29,* 131-136.

Dowdall, C. B., & Colangelo, N. (1982). Underachieving gifted students: Review and implications. *Gifted Child Quarterly, 26,* 179-184.

Drews, E.E.M., & Teahan, J. E. (1957). Parental attitudes and academic achievers. *Journal of Clinical Psychology, 13,* 382-332.

Duncan, O. D. (1961). A socioeconomic index for all occupations. In A. J. Reiss Jr. (Ed.), *Occupations and social status* (pp. 109-138). New York: Free Press.

Durr, W. K., & Collier, C. C. (1960). Recent research on the gifted. *Education, 81,* 163-169.

Dweck, C. S., & Elliot, E. S. (1983). Achievement motivation. In E. M. Hetherington (Ed.), *Handbook of child psychology* (4th ed., vol. 4, pp. 643-691). New York: John Wiley.

Farquhar, W. W., & Payne, D. A. (1964). A classification and comparison of techniques used in selecting under- and overachievers. *Personnel and Guidance Journal, 42,* 874-884.

Featherman, D. L. (1980). Schooling and occupational careers: Constancy and change in worldly success. In O. G. Brim, Jr. & J. Kagan, (Eds.), *Constancy and change in human development* (pp. 675-738). Cambridge, MA: Harvard University Press.

Fine, B. (1967). *Underachievers: How they can be helped.* New York: Dutton.

Fine, M., & Pitts, R. (1980). Intervention with underachieving gifted children: Rationale and strategies. *Gifted Child Quarterly, 24,* 51-55.

Fitzpatrick, N. (1984). Secondary III Core Program is for underachieving average ability students. *NASSP Bulletin, 68,* 94-97.

Flaugher, R. L., & Rock, D. A. (1969). A multiple-moderator approach to the identification of over- and underachievers. *Journal of Educational Measurement, 6,* 223-228.

Fliegler, L. A. (1957). Understanding the underachieving gifted child. *Psychological Reports, 3,* 533-536.

Flowers, J. V., Horsman, J., & Schwartz, B. (1982). The underachieving gifted child. In J. V. Flowers (Ed.), *Raising your gifted child*. Englewood Cliffs, NJ: Prentice-Hall.

Gerler, E. R., Bland, M., Melang, P., & Miller, D. (1986). The effect of small-group counseling on underachievers. *Elementary School Guidance & Counseling, 20,* 303-305.

Gerler, E. R., Kinney, J., & Anderson, R. F. (1985). The effects of counseling on classroom performance. *Journal of Humanistic Education and Development, 23,* 155-165.

Goldberg, M. L., Bernhard, S. J., Kirschner, S., Hlavaty, J., Michelson, B., Goldberg, C., & Apel, L. (1959). A three year experimental program at DeWitt Clinton High School to help bright underachievers. *High Points, 41,* 5-35.

Gowan, J. C. (1957). Dynamics of the underachievement of gifted students. *Exceptional Children, 24,* 98-122.

Greene, M. M. (1963). Overachieving and underachieving gifted high school girls. In L. D. Crow & A. Crow (Eds.), *Educating the academically able* (pp. 203-205). New York: David McKay.

Guerney, B. G., Jr. (Ed.). (1977). *Relationship enhancement: Skill training programs for therapy, problem prevention, and enrichment.* San Francisco: Jossey-Bass.

Gurman, A. S. (1970). The role of the family in underachievement. *Journal of School Psychology, 8,* 48-53.

Hall, E. G. (1983). Recognizing gifted underachievers. *Roeper Review, 5*(4), 23-25.

Heinemann, A. (1977). *Star power: Providing for the gifted and talented. Module 6, Underachievers among the gifted and talented.* (ERIC Document Reproduction Service No. ED176 505). Austin, TX: Education Service Center, Region B.

Hildreth, G. (1966). *Introduction to the gifted.* New York: McGraw-Hill.

Hoffman, J. L., Wasson, F. R., & Christianson, B. P. (1985). Personal development for the gifted underachiever. *G/C/T, 8,* 12-14.

Holmes, F. (1962). A study of psychological, emotional, and intellectual factors associated with achievement and underachievement. *Independent School Bulletin, 1,* 54-59.

Hout, M., & Morgan, W. R. (1975). Race and sex variations in the causes of the expected attainments of high school seniors. *American Journal of Sociology, 81,* 364-394.

Hummel, R., & Sprinthall, N. (1965). Underachievement related to interests, attitudes, and values. *Personnel and Guidance Journal, 44,* 388-398.

Humphreys, L. G. (1974). The misleading distinction between aptitude and achievement tests. In D. R. Green (Ed.), *The aptitude-achievement distinction.* Monterey, CA: CTB/McGraw-Hill.

Jackson, R. M., Cleveland, J. C., & Merenda, P. F. (1975). The longitudinal effects of early identification and counseling of underachievers. *Journal of School Psychology, 13*(2), 119-128.

Jones, E., & Gerard, H. (1967). *Foundations of social psychology.* New York: John Wiley.

Kaplan, R. M., & Saccuzzo, D. P. (1982). *Psychological testing: Principles, applications, and issues.* Pacific Grove, CA: Brooks/Cole.

Karnes, M. B., McCoy, G., Zehrbach, R. R., Wollersheim, J. P., & Clarizio, H. F. (1963). The efficacy of two organizational plans for underachieving intellectually gifted children. *Exceptional Children, 29,* 438-446.

Kehayan, V. A. (1983, March). Peer intervention network: A program for underachievers. Paper presented at the annual convention of the American Personnel and Guidance Association, Washington, DC.

Kessler, J. W. (1963). My son, the underachiever. *PTA Magazine, 58,* 12-14.

Khatena, J. (1982). *Educational psychology of the gifted.* New York: John Wiley.

Kowitz, G. T., & Armstrong, C. M. (1961). Underachievement: Concept or artifact: *School and Society, 89,* 347-349.

Krouse, J. H., & Krouse, H. J. (1981). Toward a multimodal theory of academic underachievement. *Educational Psychologist, 16,* 151-164.

Kurtz, J. J., & Swenson, S. J. (1951). Factors related to overachievement and underachievement in school. *School Review, 59,* 472-480.

Lowenstein, L. F. (1982). An empirical study of the incidence, diagnosis, treatment and follow-up of academically underachieving children. *School Psychology International, 3,* 219-230.

Mallis, J. (1983). *Diamonds in the dust: Discover and develop your child's gifts.* Austin, TX: Multi Media Arts.

Mandel, H. P., & Marcus, S. I. (1988). *The psychology of underachievement: Differential diagnosis and differential treatment.* New York: John Wiley.

Markle, A., Rinn, R. C., & Goodwin, B. (1980). Effects of achievement motivation training on academic performance of underachievers. *Psychological Reports, 47,* 567-574.

Martin, J., Marx, R. W., & Martin, E. W. (1980). Instruction counseling for chronic underachievers. *School Counselor, 28,* 109-118.

Maughan, B., Gray, G., & Rutter, M. (1985). Reading retardation and autistical behavior: A follow-up into employment. *Journal of Child Psychology and Psychiatry, 26,* 741-748.

McCall, R. B. (1983, November). Turned off & tuned out. *Parents,* pp. 104-109, 178-181.

McGuire, D. E. & Lyons, J. S. (1985). A transcontextual model for intervention with problems of school underachievement. *American Journal of Family Therapy, 13*(3), 37-45.

McIntyre, P. M. (1964). Dynamics and treatment of the passive-aggressive underachiever. *American Journal of Psychotherapy, 19,* 95-108.

Miller, L. M. (Ed.) (1961). *Guidance for the underachiever with superior ability.* (DHEW Publication No. OE-25021). Washington, DC: Government Printing Office.

Musselman, J. W. (1942). Factors associated with the achievement of high school pupils of superior intelligence. *Journal of Experimental Education, 11,* 53-68.

Myers, R. K. (1980). Underachievement in gifted pupils. (ERIC Document Reproduction Service No. ED 185 773). Proceedings of a workshop at Slippery Rock State College, Slippery Rock, PA, July 23-27, 1979.

Nelson-Le Gall, S. (1986). Personal communication.

Newman, C. J., Dember, C. F., & Krug, O. (1973). "He can but he won't": A psychodynamic study of so-called "gifted underachievers." In R. S. Eissler, A. Freud, M. Kris, & A. J. Solnit (Eds.), *The psychoanalytic study of the child* (Vol. 28, pp. 83-125). New Haven, CT: Yale University Press.

Otto, L. B., Call, V.R.A., & Spenner, K. I. (1981). *Design for a study of entry into careers.* Lexington, MA: Lexington.

O'Shea, A. J. (1970). Low-achievement syndrome among bright junior high school boys. *Journal of Educational Research, 63,* 257-262.

Overall, J. E., & Klett, C. J. (1972). *Applied multivariate analysis.* New York: McGraw-Hill.

Passow, A. H., & Goldberg, M. L. (1963). Study of underachieving gifted. In L. D. Crow & A. Crow (Eds.), *Educating the academically able* (pp. 198-202). New York: David McKay.

Pecaut, L. S. (1979). *Understanding and influencing student motivation* (Vols.1-2). Glen Ellyn, IL: Institute for Motivational Development.

Perkins, J. A., & Wicas, E. A. (1971). Group counseling bright underachievers and their mothers. *Journal of Counseling Psychology, 3,* 273-278.

Pirozzo, R. (1982). Gifted underachievers. *Roeper Review, 4,* 18-21.

Pless, T., & Satterwhite, B. (1973). A measure of family functioning and its application. *Social Science and Medicine, 1,* 613-621.

Reynolds, C. R. (1984). Critical measurement issues in learning disabilities. *Journal of Special Education, 18,* 451-477.

Richards, H. C., Gaver, D., & Golicz, H. (1984). Academically unpredictable school children: Their attitudes toward school subjects. *Journal of Educational Research, 77,* 273-276.

Rimm, S. (1984). Underachievement. *G/C/T, 31,* 26-29.

Rimm, S. (1985a). How to reach the underachiever. *Instructor, 95,* 73-76.

Rimm, S. (1985b). Identifying underachievement: The characteristics approach. *G/C/T, 41,* 2-5.

Rocks, T. G., Baker, S. B., & Guerney, B. G., Jr. (1985). Effects of counselor-directed relationship enhancement training on underachieving, poorly communicating students and their teachers. *School Counselor, 32,* 231-238.

Roth, R. M. (1970). *Underachieving students and guidance.* Boston: Houghton Mifflin.

Roth, R. M., Berenbaum, H. L., & Hershenson, D. (1967). *A developmental theory of psychotherapy: A systematic eclecticism.* Unpublished manuscript, Illinois Institute of Technology, Chicago, IL.

Roth, R. M., & Puri, P. (1967). Direction of aggression and the non-achievement syndrome. *Journal of Counseling Psychology, 14,* 277-281.

Rotheram, M. J. (1982). Social skills training with underachievers, disruptive, and exceptional children. *Psychology in the Schools, 19,* 532-539.

Runco, M. A., & Pezdek, K. (1984). The effect of television and radio on children's creativity. *Human Communications Research, 11,* 109-120.

Sahler, O.J.Z. (1983). The teenager with failing grades. *Pediatrics in Review, 4,* 293-300.

Sears, P. S., & Sherman, V. S. (1964). *In pursuit of self-esteem.* Belmont, CA: Wadsworth.

Sewell, W. H., Haller, A. O., & Ohlendorf, G. W. (1970). The educational and early occupational attainment process: Replication and revision. *American Sociological Review, 35,* 1014-1027.

Sewell, W. H., Haller, A. O., & Portes, A. (1969). The educational and early occupation attainment process. *American Sociological Review, 34,* 82-91.

Sewell, W. H., & Hauser, R. M. (1972). Causes and consequences of higher education: Models of the status attainment process. *American Journal of Agricultural Economics, 54,* 851-861.

Sewell, W. H., Hauser, R. M., & Wolf, W. C. (1980). Sex, schooling, and occupational status. *American Journal of Sociology, 86,* 551-583.

Shaw, M. C., & McCuen, J. T. (1960). The onset of academic underachievement in bright children. *The Journal of Educational Psychology, 51*(3), 103-108.

Shoff, H. G. (1984). The gifted underachiever: Definitions and identification strategies. (ERIC Document Reproduction Service No. ED 252 029). Champaign, IL: ERIC.

Slavin, R. E. (1989). Students at risk of school failure: The problem and its dimensions. In R. E. Slavin, N. L. Karweit, & N. A. Madden (Eds.), *Effective programs for students at risk* (pp. 3-19). Boston: Allyn & Bacon.

Slavin, R. E., Karweit, N. L. & Madden, N. A., Eds. (1989). *Effective programs for students at risk.* Boston: Allyn & Bacon.

Smart, W. E. (1985, January 18). In search of achievement. *Washington Post*, p. C5.

Smith, M. B. (1968). Competence and socialization. In J. A. Clausen (Ed.), *Socialization and society* (pp. 270-320). Boston: Little, Brown.

Stern, H. G. (1963). Guidance for the gifted underachiever in high school. In L. D. Crow & A. Crow (Eds.), *Educating the academically able* (pp. 192-197). New York: David McKay.

Sternberg, R. J. (1982). Lies we live by: Misapplication of tests in identifying the gifted. *Gifted Child Quarterly, 26*, 157-161.

Strang, R. (1951). Mental hygiene of gifted children. In P. Witty (Ed.), *The gifted child.* Lexington, MA: D. C. Heath.

Taylor, A. R. (1990). Behavioral subtypes of low-achieving children: Differences in school adjustment. *Journal of Applied Developmental Psychology, 11*, 487-498.

Taylor, R. G. (1964). Personality traits and discrepant achievement: A review. *Journal of Counseling Psychology, 11*, 76-82.

Teigland, J. J., Winkler, R. C., Munger, P. F., & Kranzler, G. D. (1966). Some concomitants of underachievement at the elementary school level. *Personnel and Guidance Journal, 44*, 950-955.

Thibaut, J. N., & Kelley, H. H. (1959). *The social psychology of groups.* New York: John Wiley.

Thorndike, R. L. (1963). *The concepts of over- and underachievement.* New York: Teachers College Press.

Thorndike, R. L. (1971). *Educational measurement* (2d ed.). Washington, D. C.: American Council on Education.

Topol, P., & Rexnikoff, M. (1979). Achievers and underachievers: A comparative study of fear of success, education and career goals, and conception of woman's role among high school senior girls. *Sex Roles, 5*, 85-92.

Torrance, E. P. (1962). Who is the underachiever? *NEA Journal, 58*(8), 15-17.

Trillingham, C. C., & Bonsall, M. R. (1963). The gifted underachiever. In L. D. Crow & A. Crow (Eds.), *Educating the academically able* (pp. 210-214). New York:David McKay.

Wallach, M. A., & Wing, C. W. Jr. (1969). *The talented student.* New York: Holt, Rinehart & Winston.

Westman, J. C., & Bennett, T. M. (1985). Learning impotence and the Peter Pan fantasy. *Child Psychiatry and Human Development, 15*, 153-166.

Whitmore, J. R. (1980). *Giftedness, conflict, and underachievement.* Boston, MA: Allyn & Bacon.

Willson, V. L., & Reynolds, C. R. (1985). Another look at evaluating aptitude-achievement discrepancies in the diagnosis of learning disabilities. *Journal of Special Education, 18*, 477-487.

Wood, R. (1984). Doubts about "underachievement," particularly as operationalized by Yule, Lansdown & Urbanowicz. *British Journal of Clinical Psychology, 23*, 231-232.

Yule, W. (1973). Differential progress of reading backwards and specific reading retardation. *British Journal of Educational Psychology, 43*, 244-248.

Yule, W. (1984). The operationalizing of "underachievement"—doubts dispelled. *British Journal of Clinical Psychology, 23*, 233-234.

Zilli, M. G. (1971). Reasons why the gifted adolescent underachieves and some of the implications of guidance and counseling to this problem. *Gifted Child Quarterly, 15*, 279-292.

Zuccone, C. F., & Amerikaner, M. (1986). Counseling gifted underachievers: A family systems approach. *Journal of Counseling and Development, 64*, 590-592.

Index

About the Authors

Robert B. McCall is Director of the University of Pittsburgh's Office of Child Development and Professor of Psychology. He has authored 13 textbooks and scholarly monographs, and more than 118 technical articles and book chapters on the development of intelligence in infants and children, play, imitation, high-risk infants, peer relations, and scientific methodology. From 1980 to 1989, he was a contributing editor, monthly columnist, and feature writer for *Parents* magazine. In addition to his writing, he has coproduced two series of television news features on children, youth, and families that won national media awards from the American Psychological Foundation, the American Academy of Pediatrics, and the National Council on Family Relations.

Cynthia Evahn is Senior Technical Writer/Analyst with Applied Communications in Omaha, Nebraska. At the time of this project, she was a Research Assistant at Father Flanagan's Boys Home. She managed and conducted statistical analyses on the database and reviewed portions of the literature.

Lynn Kratzer is a Postdoctoral Fellow at The Center for Research in Human Development at Concordia University in Montreal. At the time of this project, she was a graduate student in developmental psychology at the University of Pittsburgh with special interests in the social perception of disabled children. She contributed substantially to the literature review in this volume.